The Political Economy of the As

D0373356

Series Editor

Vinod K. Aggarwal
Berkeley, USA

For further volumes:
http://www.springer.com/series/7840

Huck-ju Kwon · Min Gyo Koo

Editors

The Korean Government and Public Policies in a Development Nexus, Volume 1

 Springer

Editors
Huck-ju Kwon
Min Gyo Koo
Graduate School of Public Administration
Asia Development Institute
Seoul National University
Seoul
Republic of Korea (South Korea)

ISSN 1866-6507   ISSN 1866-6515   (electronic)
ISBN 978-3-319-03321-1   ISBN 978-3-319-01098-4   (eBook)
DOI 10.1007/978-3-319-01098-4
Springer Cham Heidelberg New York Dordrecht London

Library of Congress Control Number: 2013945149

Printed on acid-free paper

Springer is part of Springer Science+Business Media (www.springer.com)

Foreword

A successful transition from a pre-modern, poor, and divided society to a modern, affluent, and integrated democracy is a very elusive goal that few countries so far from the non-Western world have achieved. Japan was the first, followed by the Asian Tigers such as Korea, Taiwan, and Singapore. Of developing countries today, China and Brazil are most determinedly implementing catch-up strategies with an impressive record of economic growth for the last two decades. For many developing countries, there must be a great deal of lessons to be gleaned from each of these successful stories.

This book is designed to look into the case of Korean development experience. Over the last five decades, Korea has successfully moved from a traditional labor-based economy to a knowledge-based one, while effectively consolidating democracy. The first-ever female President of the country took office in 2013 and Samsung competes with Apple all over the world. The welfare state in Korea has become more inclusive with a wide range of social protection programs such as public health care, pensions, and a variety of social services. The Korean experience is very much unique even among the successful transition cases to the extent that the country has achieved not only economic but also political and social development.

If one defines the development as structural transformation, the Korean case must stand out as an apt illustration. Certainly, there is a depth of the literature on the Korean development experience, but the analytical angle has been focused only on economic dimensions. A major value added of this book is that it pays particular attention to the Korean government and public policies and that it offers new insights on how the Korean government has worked effectively to drive the country forward.

The book is the first volume of a series on development and public policies that the Asia Development Institute (ADI) plans to publish for both academic and practitioner readers in the coming years. The ADI was established in 2004 with a vision to share the development experience and knowledge, and has conducted many research projects and provided high-quality trainings for policy practitioners from developing countries. The editors of this book, Dr. Huck-ju Kwon and Dr. Min Gyo Koo, also serve as ADI's Deputy Director and Research Director, respectively. Thanks to their efforts, the book benefits from the distinguished chapter writers and their in-depth research.

I anticipate that many students of development studies will read this book. One of the first cohorts of this book will be the foreign students at the Graduate School of Public Administration (GSPA), Seoul National University where the ADI is housed. In collaboration with the Korea International Cooperation Agencies, the GSPA launched a Global Master of Public Administration (GMPA) program in 2011 for future policy leaders from over 20 developing countries. A book to be widely read by future policymakers must be the one that all public policy scholars desire to write. I congratulate the authors of this book on their very stimulating and interesting contribution to our knowledge on economic and social development and am proud that the ADI plays a significant role in such a dissemination effort.

Jongwon Choi
Graduate School of Public Administration
Asia Development Institute
Seoul National University

Contents

Contents

Contributors

Byung-Sun Choi Graduate School of Public Administration, Seoul National University, Seoul, South Korea

Tobin Im Graduate School of Public Administration, Seoul National University, Seoul, South Korea

Yong-duck Jung Graduate School of Public Administration, Seoul National University, Seoul, South Korea

Shin-Bok Kim Graduate School of Public Administration, Seoul National University, Seoul, South Korea

Min Gyo Koo Graduate School of Public Administration, Seoul National University, Seoul, South Korea

Huck-ju Kwon Graduate School of Public Administration, Seoul National University, Seoul, South Korea

Chapter 1
Introduction

The Role of Government in Korea's Economic and Social Transition

Huck-ju Kwon and Min Gyo Koo

The economic growth of the Republic of Korea (hereinafter Korea) remains one of the most remarkable development stories of our time. Its growth was acheived while rapidly reducing poverty and social inequality. How did Korea transform itself from a poor and war-torn society into a modern, industrial democracy in less than 60 years? Korea's metamorphosis is indeed a rare example of a successful transition from one of the world's poorest developing countries to a highly sophisticated industrial society—an experience which many developing countries are keen to emulate. This book is designed to recapture the Korean transition by analyzing the institutional foundation of its government and public policies. As will be discussed below, the government of Korea single-mindedly carried out public policies to stimulate economic growth, but the government and public policies have themselves been affected and changed by the process. The contention of this book is that the transition of Korean society and the evolution of the Korean government are the results of two-way interactions. In this context, the book aims to analyze the way in which the dynamics of public administration were shaped within the Korean government and the kinds of public policies and instruments that were adopted to encourage this economic and social development. This analysis will allow a more complete understanding of the economic and social transformation of Korea. Surprisingly, there is a paucity of research on this aspect—a gap which this book seeks to fill.

There exists a large body of literature that attempts to explain the underlying dynamics of Korea's developmental success over the last few decades. In this literature, there are two strands of research that have evolved around two major

H. Kwon (✉) · M. G. Koo
Graduate School of Public Administration, Seoul National University, Seoul 151-742, Republic of Korea
e-mail: hkwon4@snu.ac.kr

M. G. Koo
e-mail: mgkoo@snu.ac.kr

H. Kwon and M. G. Koo (eds.), *The Korean Government and Public Policies in a Development Nexus, Volume 1*, The Political Economy of the Asia Pacific, DOI: 10.1007/978-3-319-01098-4_1, © Springer International Publishing Switzerland 2014

debates on economic development. The first strand centers around the role of the state and the market. In the early debate on economic development in East Asia—which includes Korea, Taiwan, Hong Kong, and Singapore—commentators such as Balassa argued that the economic success of the so-called Asian Tigers was market-driven, while the state only provided necessary infrastructure to enable industry to function efficiently with minimum interference (Balassa 1981).

This view was soon challenged by a second strand of research that emphasized the importance of the role of the state. In particular, Amsden maintained that the Korean state intervened in the market by getting relative prices "wrong" so that Korean exporters could have an advantageous position in the international market (Amsden 1989). Furthermore, Amsden pointed out, the strong discipline that the Korean state demanded of large conglomerates made state intervention unique. In other words, the state in Korea regulated social actors to do the job, rather than doing it on its own. For instance, the state enforced high performance standards on private firms, rewarding those that met its standards and sanctioning those that failed. Other scholars, such as Woo-Cummings, borrowed Chalmers Johnson's famous notion of the developmental state to capture the characteristics of the state in Korea (Woo-Cumings 1999). The developmental state mobilized available resources for economic development, while other social priorities were continually considered as secondary to its economic purpose.

There is also a large body of studies by Korean scholars that looks into the role of the Korean state. The work of SaKong and Jones deals with government and business relations to focus attention on the role of entrepreneurship in the private sector (SaKong and Jones 1980), while Song highlights the role of the state in the rise of Korea's economy (Song 1990). In a nutshell, the literature in this strand points out that the state in Korea intervened in the market in a particular way so that market actors did their job effectively for economic development. For instance, the Korean state did not produce automobiles through nationalized firms, which is a typical mode of state intervention, but nurtured and regulated private enterprises to produce automobiles. In order to capture these different modes of state intervention, Kwon contrasts the role of the state with the concepts of provider and regulator (Kwon 1997).

While the first strand of research was carried out to understand the nature of state-market relations in the process of Korea's transition, the second strand has examined the political dynamics of this transition. In the latter case, specific attention has been paid to the characteristics of the Korean state as a driving force for development. According to Kohli, who points out the legacy of the colonial state (Kohli 2004), the cohesive-capitalist state—which was very effective in organizing social actors for economic development—had, in fact, been established under Japanese rule. While it is certainly true that the colonial state left its legacies immediately after liberation in 1945, it remains controversial whether or not these colonial legacies played a key role in Korea's early industrialization from the mid-1960s to the 1970s.

One of the most important political events that shaped the characteristics and capability of the Korean state was the military coup d'état by Park Chung-hee in

1961. Following the coup, the military government made it clear that economic development was its top priority, and embarked on an ambitious economic development plan. After the first 2 years, when the Supreme Council of National Reconstruction—a sort of ruling military junta—governed the country, the new government was established in 1963 under a fresh constitution that established a strong presidency. Before the 1963 election, General Park justified his military coup and indicated his future policy direction (Park 1963, p. 177).

> I want to emphasize and reemphasize that the key factor of the May 16th Military Revolution was in effect an industrial revolution in Korea. Since the primary objective of the revolution was to achieve a national renaissance, the revolution envisaged political, social, and cultural reform as well. My chief concern, however, was economic revolution.

In 1963, Park was elected president of the Third Republic. Although in theory the presidential system did not contradict the principle of democracy, opposition forces were ruthlessly oppressed, and—if necessary—were accused of being communist infiltrators. In 1972, Park amended the constitution again to enable himself to become president for life, with his regime subsequently turning into an outright authoritarian one. The ugly side of the Park government is one feature of the Korean state, but there is another feature as well. As already discussed, the policy regime of the Park government is characterized by the notion of the developmental state in which elite policymakers pursue economic development as an overarching goal, and an effective bureaucracy supports this goal (Kwon 2005). The Korean developmental state worked tirelessly since the mid-1960s for economic development. Aside from its harsh oppression of opposition groups, the state controlled capital flows and nurtured strategic industries for export. Korea's business conglomerates, commonly known as *chaebol*, were highly dependent on credit supplied by state-controlled banks and thus had to comply with the government's industrial policies and guidelines. Recent work by Kim and Vogel (2011) shows this two-sided nature of the developmental state. In the broad context of development, the hypothesis that authoritarian government is necessary for developing countries to achieve economic growth has been around for some time (Domínguez 2011). Although the Park government may have supported the developmental dictatorship hypothesis, it seems to miss the point. Many authoritarian governments have failed to take their countries forward and, instead, have often created political chaos and dismal economic conditions. The crux of the matter lies in how the government delivers policies to achieve economic and social growth.

Studies focusing on the relationship between the Korean state and market have contributed to an understanding of the country's rapid transition from a poor economy to an industrialized one, while other studies, focusing on Korean politics, have provided a better perception of the political nature of the state. Nevertheless, it is fair to say that these studies fall short of providing an insight into how the Korean government was organized in practice to deliver public policies and services. It is partly because the studies have focused on macro-level variables, such as the state and the market, that they have not provided adequate explanations for institutions and public policies at the mezzo-level. In short, they have not given a clearer understanding of how the Korean state has delivered economic and social benefits at the ground level.

The aim of this book is to unpack the Korean government and its public policies by looking into the government's inner workings. The authors' contention is that this knowledge can be readily used by policymakers and development practitioners elsewhere in the world. The book is structured in two parts, each with three chapters. Part I deals with government and coordination for development, and sets out to examine the way in which different ministries and agencies were organized and coordinated with each other on economic development, especially through effective presidential leadership as well as bureaucratic initiative.

Chapter 2 by Yong-duck Jung analyzes the institutional characteristics of the presidential executive leadership. As previous studies emphasize, the role of President Park in the pursuit of economic development was crucial, but he was only part of the institutional configuration of—in Jung's term—an "institutional presidency." This chapter examines how executive leadership has been practiced in terms of political accountability, democratic representativeness, and political capability. Jung divides the institutional presidency into three components: the president, the presidential secretariat (PS), and central agencies (CAs) of the government. The PS comprises staff in the presidential office who provides the president with policy advice. The CAs are ministries, agencies and offices that perform functions essential to coordination throughout the government. In the pre-Park era, as well as in the early years of the Third Republic, which was formed in December 1962 under Park's leadership, the PS and CAs were neither strong nor fully established. As a result, the president had to resort to his personal charisma and leadership capacity in order to reconstruct his war-torn country. Once the Park government was consolidated in the mid-1960s, the institutional presidency began to evolve.

The changes and continuities in the institutional presidency can be divided into three periods. The first period was from the late 1940s to the early 1960s, when institutionalization of the presidential secretariat was weak. In the second period, from the late 1960s to the late 1980s, the core executive was developed and acquired greater power. In the third period, from the late 1980s to the present, the institutional presidency began to pose a dilemma, and there has been a strong call for reducing the power of the institutional presidency as well as the continual need for executive leadership for effective policymaking and implementation. During the period of Korea's transition, Jung argues that the institutional presidency was able to stand above other government structures, thus maintaining the common interests of government ministries and consistency in public policies.

Chapter 3 by Byung-Sun Choi analyzes one of the most important CAs during the developmental period, namely, the Economic Planning Board (EPB). Created in 1961, the EPB had the authority to determine long-term economic development planning while maintaining coordination and consistency across government agencies. Choi claims that the successful economic development of Korea would have been impossible without the EPB. He also argues that effective and competent economic policymaking and coordination are more important than economic development plans themselves because unanticipated bottlenecks, obstacles, problems, or new investment opportunities need to be addressed properly and wisely once the initial stage for economic growth is set.

For Choi, the factor that made the EPB so unique and special in performing its mission was not simply the putting together of planning and budgeting functions in one organization, but the exploitation of its institutional autonomy that led it to possess a broader and longer-term perspective, and enjoy a higher degree of flexibility in making economic policy choices. This turned out to be instrumental in steering the course of economic development in the direction deemed most desirable, in the face of turns and twists of economic and political developments both within and outside Korea. Most notably, Choi maintains, the EPB had to strenuously earn the support of the president for its activities in a never-ending policy competition among related ministries through the adroit and strategic management of its political mandate, and through an extraordinary effort to build up its own unique organizational capacity and competence. Even though the president and core executive agencies set up overall policy, and maintained consistency within the government, it was the line ministries that carried out public policies in their respective fields. For this reason, it is crucial to organize line ministries in a way that enables them to do their job effectively. The role of the state in economic development and transition has been discussed extensively in the literature mentioned above. However, the organizational dimension of this process has not been adequately studied. Existing scholarship has made large assumptions about the organizational nature of the Korean government, thus providing an incomplete picture of the depth and breadth of the government's organizational landscape.

Chapter 4 by Tobin Im approaches this topic from the perspective of classical organization theory and sheds new light on the distinctive aspects of Korea's government as a collection of various organizations. Im points out that in existing scholarship, the nature of organizations in the Korean government has been obscured by a misplaced emphasis on organizational principles developed and tailor-made for Western governments. Currently, there exists a large gap between what students of public administration learn about the Western principles of organizational management and how the Korean bureaucracy has actually operated in the past and is currently operating. As such, this chapter raises fundamental questions about the universal applicability and validity of Western organization theory. Im does not deny the fact that Western theories and principles of public organizations have had a positive impact on Korea's public administration and organization. Nevertheless, what is fundamentally more important for him is that the Korean government has evolved along historical pathways that are embedded in Korea's native principles of efficiency and competitiveness.

While Part I examines how the Korean government has evolved in the process of economic and social development, Part II explores prominent public policies that the Korean government implemented during its developmental period. Chapter 5, on "Governing the Developmental Welfare State: From Regulation to Provision" by Huck-ju Kwon, analyzes social policy in Korea with a special focus on the mode of state intervention. Kwon argues that social protection was only a subordinate part of the overall policy paradigm for economic development. He characterizes the way social policies and institutions were arranged as the developmental welfare state. In explaining its mode of intervention, Kwon contrasts the role of the state as regulator with that of the state as provider. Within the mode of regulator in the delivery of social policy, the state issues regulations under which other social actors deliver social protection. By contrast, in the mode of provider the state actually delivers social services and benefits which are then paid for through state expenditure. Kwon shows the different attributes of the two modes of state intervention, but his main point is that the policy regime of regulator has allowed the Korean state to mobilize limited resources for economic development, while putting the responsibility of social protection on families, employers, and civil organizations.

An important question that arises from this analysis is how Korean society managed to keep social inequality at a minimum during its period of rapid economic growth. According to Kwon, the Korean government was able to set up this policy regime and implement social policies because there were multifunctional institutions that indirectly served to implement them. For instance, land reform—which was carried out in the late 1940s and early 1950s—was an effective social policy, helping transform indigent peasants to self-owning farmers and assuring them of a basic livelihood on small but adequate agricultural land. Local health centers which were established across rural areas were able to provide the poor with essential health care with minimal facilities. Interestingly, these local health centers were operated by young trainee doctors who worked there in lieu of military service. Among other examples that Kwon puts forward is the *saemaul undong* (or New Village Movement) of the 1970s, a sort of self-help voluntary community movement which was implemented nationwide. It mobilized human and economic resources for rural communities, and improved the infrastructure of agricultural and rural industries.

In 2011, Korea became the ninth country to join the "one-trillion-dollar trading club," departing from the ranks of newly emerging countries to join the ranks of trade giants. After reaching the $100 million mark in 1964, Korea's exports grew more than 5,000 times in 47 years, making it the seventh-largest exporting country in the world. In Chap. 6, Min Gyo Koo attempts to link past policy trajectories to present public policy by analyzing Korea's trade policy transformation from mercantilism to liberalism. As Koo points out, Korea's economic development model has been characterized as export-oriented industrialization (EOI), or a mercantilist policy centered on export promotion and import protection. For the past two decades, however, Korea's trade policy has undergone fundamental change, as illustrated by its active pursuit of free trade agreements. This is particularly important because, in an era of globalization and democratization, Korea's EOI can no longer be replicated in other parts of the world. At the same time, however, the centrality of the Korean state in the process of trade liberalization should be recognized.

The significance of Korea's trade policy transformation is threefold. First, it constitutes a notable policy shift from developmental mercantilism to liberalism. Second, it has been shaped by a top-down political initiative rather than a bottom-up demand from business groups and the general public. And third, despite Korea's liberal but state-centric nature, its partisan politics has led its trade policy to be closely embedded in the country's social fabric, both competitive and noncompetitive. As such, Koo argues that Korea's new trade policy adopts "developmental liberalism" as opposed to "developmental mercantilism," that is, greater trade openness in favor of internationally competitive sectors and generous side payments to those who might be hurt by trade liberalization. Institutionally, the Office of the Minister for Trade (OMT) has played a vital role in this dramatic change. As a champion of liberal economic ideas, the OMT is relatively insulated from pressure from special interest groups. As Koo indicates, the institutional design and operation of the OMT in trade issue areas resembles the EPB in broader economic policy during the 1960s–1980s.

Chapter 7, dealing with "Educational Policy, Development of Education, and Economic Growth in Korea" by Shin-Bok Kim, examines the rapid expansion of education in the early stages of economic takeoff, with a well-educated workforce on relatively low wages contributing to this takeoff. How was Korea, once one of the poorest countries, able to expand its education so rapidly? Kim explains that the role of the Korean state in education during the period of development was minimal in terms of financial commitment. Public expenditure shared only a small portion of the entire education spending. Parents took on a large part of the cost of education for their children, and their financial responsibility relieved the government of a considerable, and recurrent, burden. Also, private institutions in tertiary education provided most of the educational places for students (more than 75 %) compared to public universities. In education, the state played the role of regulator, working—as in social policy—with other actors. The downside of Korea's education policy was that educational conditions, such as facilities, the number of students per class, and the ratio of students to teachers, were relatively poor.

Despite these conditions, Korean society has been altogether successful in educating its children and accumulating human capital. Kim summarizes the significant characteristics of Korean education. First, Confucian ethics played a vital role in recognizing the importance of education and respecting teachers and scholars. Second, educational achievement was considered important in life, and not only for productive enhancement in personal development. Third, educational success led to upward mobility and to privileged positions in society.

In this book, the authors attempt to unravel the inner workings of the government and public policy to explain the transition of Korean society from one of the poorest to one of the more sophisticated industrial democracies. The development discourse of the last five decades has made clear that one size does not fit all. One cannot simply import the experience of Korea's transformation to one's own country. This book shows that it is necessary to maintain consistency and coherence in government and public policy in order to achieve economic and social transformation.

References

Amsden, A. H. (1989). *Asia's next giant: South Korea and late industrialization*. New York, NY: Oxford University Press.

Balassa, B. A. (1981). *Structural adjustment policies in developing economies*. World bank staff working paper no. 464. Washington, DC: World Bank.

Domínguez, J. (2011). The Perfect Dictatorship? South Korea versus Argentina, Brazil, Chile and Mexico. In B. -K. Kim & E. Vogel (Eds.), *The Park Chung Hee Era: The Transformation of South Korea*. Cambridge: Harvard University Press.

Kim, B.-K., & Vogel, E. F. (Eds.). (2011). *The Park Chung Hee Era: The Transformation of South Korea*. Cambridge, MA: Harvard University Press.

Kohli, A. (2004). *State-directed development: Political power and industrialization in the global periphery*. New York, NY: Cambridge University Press.

Kwon, H. (1997). Beyond European welfare regimes: Comparative perspectives on East Asian welfare systems. *Journal of Social Policy, 26*(4), 467–484.

Kwon, H. (2005). Transforming the developmental welfare state in East Asia. *Development and Change, 36*(3), 477–497.

Park, C. (1963). *The Country, the Revolution, and I*. Seoul: Hollym.

SaKong, Il, & Jones, L. P. (1980). *Government, business and entrepreurship in economic development: The korean case*. Cambridge, MA: Harvard University Press.

Song, B.-N. (1990). *The Rise of the Korean economy*. New York, NY: Oxford University Press.

Woo-Cumings, M. (Ed.). (1999). *The Developmental state*. Ithaca, NY: Cornell University Press.

Part I
Government and Coordination for Development

Chapter 2
Institutional Presidency and National Development

Yong-duck Jung

2.1 Introduction

As early as the late seventeenth century, Locke (1689) advocated political pluralism by rejecting any absolute, unified, and uncontrolled state power. Unlike
Hobbes (1651), another English philosopher of the time, who argued that vesting
absolute power in the government would be necessary to avoid an anarchic "war
of all against all," Locke contended that the state should rest on consent and that
governing authorities should never have absolute or monistic power. This stance of
political pluralism was not something that the Korean people were familiar with
when they started rebuilding a new nation state in the late 1940s.

Since the second half of the nineteenth century, Korea has followed a version
of "modernization from above" and has thereby been similar to the "late indus-
trializing countries" such as Germany and Japan. Since then, the country's modernization process has been initiated mainly by political and bureaucratic elites,
with the strong influence of foreign powers, but without any consensus building
from the common people (Jung 2005). Thus, a strong bureaucratic state was first
institutionalized, which then initiated state-led industrialization while marginaliz-
ing democratic institutions. It was in the latter years of the twentieth century that
such "limping" or "unbalanced" modernization began to turn for the better amid
booming industrialization and the development of civil society. Since the foundation of the Republic of Korea—for the first time in its history— in 1948, the

An earlier version of this chapter, entitled "The Evolution of Institutional Presidency in Korea,
1948–2011," was presented by the author at an inaugural convention of the Association for the
Study of Political Society on November 27–28, 2010, at Waseda University, Tokyo, and published in the *Japanese Review of Political Society, 1*(1), 27–44, 2012.

Y. Jung (✉)
Graduate School of Public Administration, Seoul National University,
Seoul 151-742, Republic of Korea
e-mail: ydjung@snu.ac.kr

country achieved state building (1940s–1950s), industrialization (1960s–1980s), and democratization (1990s–2000s). In the process of its development in such a relatively short period of time, the state administration has played a leading role and, by its nature, the president's executive leadership has been one of the most important factors.

In general, the country's executive leadership is supported by the constitution and other ordinances. It is also supported by diversely institutionalized core executive apparatuses, including the presidential secretariat (PS) and the central agencies (CA).[1] Through these staff organizations, the chief executive intervenes in the activities of various levels of administrative apparatuses within the executive branch. In Western industrialized countries, the core executive apparatuses had become more positively institutionalized after the mid-twentieth century, when the state's growth made it difficult to steer and coordinate the differentiated administrative apparatuses (Rose 1984; Dunleavy and Rhodes 1990; Burke 1992; Peters et al. 2000). Although Korea's First Republic was launched in 1948, the country was—in practice—a type of Asiatic administrative state, with executive predominance as well as concentration of power within the executive branch from the very beginning (Jung and Kim 2007). In this context, it is important to illuminate how Korea's executive leadership has been institutionalized since its foundation.

The institutionalization of the executive leadership is related to public values such as political responsiveness and administrative competence. In a democratic society, for example, the president's executive leadership should be practiced for political accountability and democratic representativeness (Finer 1941; Kaufman 1956; Rockman 1984; Aberbach 1990; Moe 1993). It is supported by laws, but should also be constrained by them. It is expected that the presidential executive leadership also be practiced without undermining the bureaucracy's neutral competence, which may "entail the application of bureaucratic expertise in an objective manner to obtain the best outcomes possible" (Kaufman 1956; Heclo 1975; Dickinson 1997; Meier 1997; Goodsell 2004), and contribute to long-term national interests by enhancing the state's autonomy and "plan rationality" (Johnson 1982).

This chapter intends to analyze the changes in, and continuity of, the institutional characteristics of the presidential executive leadership in Korea during the past six decades. It will also discuss how executive leadership has been practiced, reflecting public values such as political accountability, democratic representativeness and responsiveness, the neutral competence of administrative bureaucracy, policy capabilities, and so on.

---

[1] Central agencies are generally defined as the "departments, agencies, and offices [that] perform the functions [which are] essential to the co-ordination and control of bureaucracy throughout government" (Campbell and Szablowski 1979, 2). In this article, central agencies and the presidential secretariat are differentiated from each other. They have evolved separately as core executive apparatuses to support the presidential leadership in Korea (Jung et al. 2011).

2.2 Institutional Arrangements for Executive Leadership

Korea has maintained a presidential executive system for more than 60 years, with the only exception being a short-lived parliamentary government from 1960 to 1961. The Constitution of the United States (US), which has maintained a presidential system from the start, declares that only the president is bestowed with executive authority. Unlike the US constitution, the Constitution of the Republic of Korea mentions specifically the power of the president and policy apparatuses over the executive branch (Jung et al. 2011). Based on this constitutional foundation, the Korean government has institutionalized a set of complex core executive apparatuses to support the president's executive leadership.

This complex institutionalization has been caused partly by the nation's unique political executive system. The Korean government has maintained a presidential system with some parliamentary executive factors, though it is different from the dual executive system in France. The prime minister is appointed by the president, who is directly elected by the people, and "assists the president and receives the president's orders to supervise each executive ministry" (The Constitution, Article 86). Though the prime minister needs the confirmation of the national assembly to take office, he or she is—in reality—appointed chiefly in accordance with the president's will. Therefore, the prime minister maintains a position as a member of the president's staff. This dualism makes Korea's core executive apparatuses affiliated not only with the president, but also with the prime minister. The apparatuses include the PS, the prime minister's office (PM's office), and the CAs—all of which are in charge of the core executive or administrative functions headed by the chief executive (Jung et al. 2011).

2.2.1 The Presidential Secretariat: de facto "inner cabinet"?

The PS is the central staff organization of the chief executive in any presidential system, but differs greatly according to country and period (Jung et al. 2010). In Korea, the degree of differentiation of the PS had been low from the commencement of the Syngman Rhee administration (1948–1960) to the end of the first term of Chunghee Park (1963–1967) (Fig. 2.1). During this period, the PS took care merely of the PS's internal administrative affairs, protocol, public relations, and so forth.

It was at the beginning of President Park's second term in 1968 that the PS began to be greatly differentiated functionally and was expanded in size by the creation of various sub-organizations for different public policy areas. Most secretarial positions were upgraded to senior secretarial positions, to be on par with ministers or vice ministers. This change occurred with the launching of the second 5-Year Economic Development Plan (1967–1971). During the period from 1968 to 1971, the office of the senior secretary for economic affairs, for example, was differentiated into three senior secretary offices which were separately in charge of the general economy, transportation, health and welfare, liquidation of insolvent

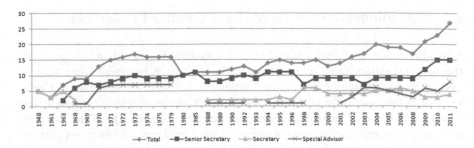

Fig. 2.1 Intraorganizational changes in the presidential secretariat, 1948–2011. *Source* Based on data from Jung et al. (2002), the *Donga-Ilbo* (http://www.donga.com) and the presidential office (www.president.go.kr/kr/index.php)

enterprises, and foreign debt management. When his third term was launched in 1972, President Park reorganized the senior secretary offices into the Senior Secretary for Economic Affairs I (covering finance and the economy, agriculture and forestry, commerce and industry, and construction); the Senior Secretary for Economic Affairs II (science and technology); and the Senior Secretary for Economic Affairs III (tourism promotion).

In addition, several special advisors were appointed for diplomacy, politics, education and culture, society, inspection and investigation, and so on. These positions were transformed into senior secretary ranks in 1980 by President Doo-hwan Chun (1980–1988). Unlike special advisors who worked with the aid of only a few administrative assistants, the senior secretaries—as chiefs of their offices—were given the support of a large number of staff members, including secretaries at the director-general level (Grades I to III). These senior secretary offices, as differentiated by policy areas, have been partially restructured, depending on the president, but the basic format has been maintained to show its durability.

The differentiations of the PS can be explained by state-led national development policies which have been conducted aggressively in Korea. Since the early 1960s, the Korean government has established a large number of economic and industrial administrative apparatuses to assertively implement its developmental policies. To incorporate these differentiated organizations into an overall national policy, the PS was enlarged and strengthened, especially since the late 1960s.

The senior secretaries to the president have been in charge of several related administrative apparatuses, and the steering of their policymaking and implementation has been conducted in a top-down way. Currently, the senior secretary to the president for economic affairs, for instance, is in charge of at least six ministerial level organizations, including the Ministry of Strategy and Finance; the Ministry of Food, Agriculture, Forestry and Fisheries; the Ministry of Knowledge Economy; the Ministry of Land, Transport and Maritime Affairs; the Fair Trade Commission; and the Financial Services Commission. The senior secretaries work closely with the president in terms of distance and communication, and have always had greater decision-making power compared to personnel of other administrative organizations. As an example, although there are individual differences, most of the ministers who wish to discuss a policy issue with the president must first discuss it with the relevant senior secretary, who then decides on the theme of the meeting, and also attends the meeting. This decision-making process has given the PS significant autonomy, similar to a de facto "inner Cabinet." The top-down structure of the PS has been maintained ever since, with some meaningful changes (Jung et al. 2010).

First, the more the PS has been differentiated and expanded, the greater has been the need for functional integration and coordination. As indicated in the previous paragraph, each senior secretary has managed several ministries and agencies of a related policy area. This has meant that the senior secretary has tended to represent the policy perspectives of the latter. As the complexity of the secretariat has increased, the difficulties of policy coordination have taken place not only within the cabinet (i.e., between ministries or agencies) but also within the PS (i.e., between secretarial offices). This had led President Young-sam Kim (1993–1998) to set up an office of senior secretary for policy planning to horizontally coordinate the secretarial offices. However, the attempt to facilitate policy coordination within the PS was not effective, and the senior secretary for policy planning had to maintain his position by initiating new tasks that did not particularly interest other senior secretaries. President Moo-hyun Roh (2003–2008) attempted to resolve that problem more vigorously by upgrading the senior secretary for policy planning to the chief of policy staff, in charge of coordinating between senior secretaries. Since then, the double-headed system of the PS, comprising the chief of staff and the chief of policy staff, has been institutionalized, resulting in the PS operating hierarchically rather than collegially. The chief of staff has had overall responsibility for the traditional secretariat, including internal administrative affairs and protocol, public relations, political affairs, foreign and national security affairs, and so forth, while the chief of policy staff has had overall responsibility for coordinating domestic policies.

Second, the PS has been continually faced with legitimacy issues, accused of having a negative image, exercising authoritarianism, or being a "center of power politics." When President Syngman Rhee resigned following accusations that he was undemocratic, his PS—which dealt at that time mostly with protocol and political, not policy, affairs—was perceived in an unfavorable light as the basic power center of an authoritarian regime. President Bo-seon Yoon (1960–1962), under the parliamentary executive system, attempted to change the adverse image of the presidential residence and office by altering its name from *Gyeongmudae*, which had some connotations of a royal palace, to *Cheongwadae*, or "Blue House". However, from the presidency of Park (especially from 1972 to 1979) to that of President Chun, when authoritarianism mostly deepened in Korea, the negative image of the PS as the center of authoritarian power politics became more entrenched. Since the democratic transition of 1987, the tendency has been for an incumbent administration to attempt to display its democratic characteristics by diminishing the size and role of the PS. All of the succeeding presidents after the democratic transition have sought to reduce the size of the secretariat

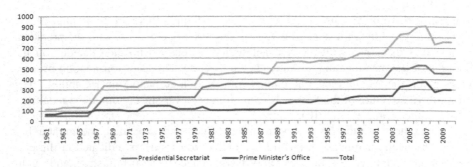

Fig. 2.2 Number of staff in the presidential secretariat and prime minister's office, 1961–2010. *Source* Updated from Jung et al. (2002)

and decentralize policymaking and coordination power by delegating these to the prime minister and other ministers at the beginning of their administration. But the size and role of the PS was eventually to grow in later years (Fig. 2.2).

2.2.2 The Prime Minister and His Office: de facto "political bulletproof vest"?

There are, formally, only a few organizations directly responsible to the president, including the Board of Audit and Inspection, the National Intelligence Service, and a few advisory committees. Except for them, most of the core executive apparatuses, including the CAs, have been institutionalized under the prime minister. Nevertheless, the heads of these organizations are appointed and directed by the president, and they also directly report to the president without having to first consult with the prime minister. Even the PM's office—the only staff organization to directly assist the prime minister—has not been free from the influence of the PS. For example, the head of the PM's office has been customarily appointed by the president (Jung 1996).

Such a passive and limited role of the prime minister may receive mixed assessments in Korea. In reality, the president makes decisions on, and coordinates most of, the important public policies. But when a policy fails, the prime minister and his office are held responsible. The inconsistency of the prime minister's real and nominal roles and the resulting "inconsistency of power and accountability" have received much criticism (Cho and Im 2010). Even so, it may be possible to also view this inconsistency in a positive light, that is, the prime minister's taking responsibility for most policy failures instead of the president—including cases of his or her resignation, depending on the severity of the issue—has in fact contributed to political stability in Korea. This is proven by the fact that from 1948 to 2008, 9 Korean presidents have had an average term of 6.4 years, while the 38 prime ministers have had an average term of only 1.3 years (Fig. 2.3).

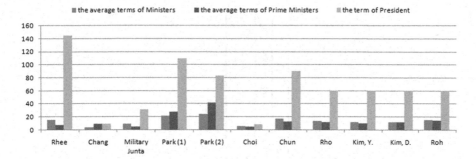

Fig. 2.3 Average terms of ministers, prime ministers, and presidents by administration, 1948–2008. *Note* A unit is 1 month. *Source* Based on data from the Ministry of Government Administration and Home Affairs (MOGAHA) (1998) and websites of the prime minister's office and each of the ministries

As such, Korean prime ministers have acted mostly as a "political bulletproof vest" to protect the president by using symbolic politics. In addition to this role, there are a few other roles that have also been played by the prime minister with the assistance of the PM's office. These include regulatory reforms and performance evaluations—two major functions that are legally stipulated—as well as some minor level policy coordination between ministries or agencies. While most of the important policy issues have been carried out directly by the president and the PS, those that could be politically risky for the president, or carry high opportunity costs, are mostly delegated to the prime minister and the PM's office.

As if to reveal its real position, the legal base of the PM's office has been vague until now (Jung et al. 2011). The role of the PM's office was relatively significant when a prime minister was politically or personally close to a president, as in the case of Prime Ministers Jong-pil Kim (1971–1975), Jae-bong Rho (1990–1991), and Hea-chan Lee (2004–2006) (Han 2010). But even in these instances, the delegated authority was temporary and due largely to the political need of the president. If the prime minister challenged the president in any way, he could scarcely keep his position.

Since the democratic transition in 1987, Korean presidents have been criticized for practicing an "imperial presidency" or chief executive predominance within the executive branch. This has made them respond in one of two ways. First, presidents tend to rely more on the symbolic uses of politics. For example, when President Tae-woo Rho (1988–1993) participated in cabinet meetings, with the prime minister seated next to him, he—along with other cabinet members—would remove his jacket and roll up his shirtsleeves to present an atmosphere that was both practical and democratic to the press. Regardless of this unusual political gesture, the rate of his participation in cabinet meetings was the lowest (Table 2.1).

Second, after the 1987 democratic transition, presidents have been inclined to decentralize decision making and entrust it to the prime minister and the PM's office—at least on the surface—in the hope of proving their democratic

Table 2.1 Participation of presidents in all cabinet meetings by administration, 1949–2001

President	Rhee			Park-1				Park-2	Chun			Rho		Y. Kim			D. Kim	
Year	1949	1953	1956	1958	1965	1968	1970	1974	1976	1982	1984	1986	1988	1992	1993	1995	1997	1999	2001
Proportion (%) of participation	66.0	71.0	38.0	35.8	3.5	4.0	10.2	16.8	6.1	7.2	3.7	5.4	2.0	1.8	9.8	6.0	3.4	73.5	83.9

Source Based on data from Chung (1994) and the National Archive (http://www.archives.go.kr/)

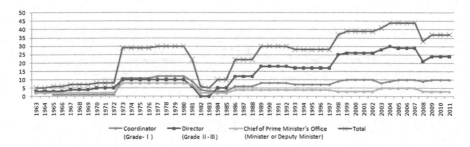

Fig. 2.4 Intraorganizational changes in the prime minister's office, 1963–2011

credentials, and hence the legitimacy of their administration. For example, the PM's office came to serve as a secretariat for the vice ministerial meetings since 1994, the Presidential Commission on Administrative Reform (1993–1998), the Regulatory Reform Committee (1998–present), and the Government Performance Evaluation Committee since 1998 (Jung 2007). The addition of these functions to the PM's office, with legal bases, has enhanced substantially not only its differentiation but also its autonomy and durability (Figs. 2.2 and 2.4)

The administration of the incumbent President, Myung-bak Lee (2008–2013), reduced the policy coordinating functions of the PM's office in the name of "small government". However, it can also be evaluated as a reform to normalize Korea's dualistic structure of the roles of the president and prime minister. In accordance with this change, Prime Minister Seung-soo Han (2008–2009) played an even more limited role than his predecessors, often visiting foreign countries for overseas energy diplomacy. It was only 2 months after the inauguration of his term, however, that the Lee administration realized anew the need for a "political bulletproof vest" role for the prime minister. Since the administration faced fierce civil protests that erupted during the Korea–US Free Trade Association negotiations on beef imports, the role of the prime minister and the PM's office have been expanding again (Figs. 2.2 and 2.4)

2.2.3 Central Agencies: "Standardizing" Core Administrative Functions

A number of CAs with the title of "board," "ministry," "agency," or "office" have been organized and reorganized either directly under the president or the prime minister (Fig. 2.5). Each CA carries out the standardization of core administrative functions which are essential to the operation of administrative apparatuses. These include policy planning, coordinating, budgeting, organizing, staffing, central–local relations, legislating, public relations, performance evaluation, audit and inspection, and so on. By intervening in the operations of all administrative apparatuses through these standardizations, the CAs ultimately support, directly or indirectly, the executive leadership of the president.

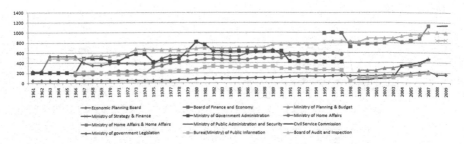

Fig. 2.5 Organizational configurations and staffing of central agencies, 1948–2010. *Note* The police force is excluded from the Ministry of Home Affairs. *Source* Based on data from Yoo and Lee (2010), MOGAHA (1998) and the Board of Audit and Inspection (2008)

Since the CAs standardize and control key administrative functions essential to the operation of administrative apparatuses, the latter are inevitably subordinate to the former in terms of real authority. As Campbell and Szablowski (1979, 2) note, the CAs "stand above other departments in that they perform functions which are thought to be crucial to the *common* interests of government departments, and which relate to matters of major importance".

Moreover, the personnel of some of the CAs had been given positions or grades on par with, or higher than, ordinary administrative apparatuses. For example, the ministers of the Economic Planning Board (1961–1994) and its succeeding Board of Finance and Economy (1994–1998) were given the rank of deputy prime minister, a position higher than that of other ministers (Jung et al. 2011). The personnel (bureau directors) of the Board of Audit and Inspection have been provided with a higher grade than those in comparable posts (bureau directors) in other ministries. These higher grades or positions put the staff of the CAs on a more elevated level than those in other administrative apparatuses in their interactions. The CAs continue to work closely with various senior secretaries to the president, or the president himself, and effectively support the president by standardizing and controlling crucial administrative functions of other administrative apparatuses.

Since the early 1990s, when the administrative reform process set out to achieve "small government," some CAs were integrated into related ministries with line functions so that a single ministry could conduct both line and staff functions. For example, the Economic Planning Board was merged with the Ministry of Finance to form the Board of Finance and Economy in 1994, and the Ministry of Government Administration was amalgamated with the Ministry of Home Affairs to form the Ministry of Government Administration and Home Affairs (1998). But they were differentiated again, even when the structural adjustment of the public sector was conducted soon after the foreign liquidity crisis of 1997. As a result, the Board of Finance and Economy became, in 1998, the Ministry of Planning and Budget and the Ministry of Finance and Economy, while the personnel administration functions of the Ministry of Government Administration and Home Affairs were hived off into the newly created Civil Service Commission in 1999. In February 2008, when the current administration of Myung-bak Lee took office, another minor small government-oriented restructuring took place, resulting in the Ministry of Planning and Budget and the Ministry of Finance and Economy being combined to form the Ministry of Strategy and Finance, and the Ministry of Government Administration and Home Affairs, the Civil Service Commission, and the Emergency Planning Commission joining to form the Ministry of Public Administration and Security. Regardless of these changes in organizational configuration and size, the CAs have maintained their durability over the past six decades (Jung et al. 2011).

2.3 Periodical Characteristics of Presidential Leadership

The six decades of institutionalization analyzed in the preceding sections can be grouped into three typical periods of around two decades, more or less, reflecting Korea's national development process of state-building, industrialization, and democratization—in that order. The institutional characteristics and performance in regard to public values of the presidential executive leadership of the three periods are discussed below (Sects. 2.3.1, 2.3.2, and 2.3.3)

2.3.1 Passive Institutionalization of the Core Executive: Late 1940s to Early 1960s

During its first stage, from the late 1940s to the early 1960s, the PS was not very institutionalized, as indicated above (Figs. 2.1 and 2.6). This can be explained by President Rhee's personal leadership style. He would say that in a country with a presidential executive system—as can be inferred from the use of the term "secretary" (for "minister") as in the US—the ministers were merely administrative aides to the president, unlike in countries with a parliamentary executive system where the cabinet consisted of mainly senior parliamentary members. As an incomparable political leader with outstanding knowledge of policy, President Rhee practiced executive leadership by mobilizing personal networks from both home and abroad with great charisma, and by communicating directly with ministers within the executive branch.[2]

---

[2] Syngman Rhee was a pioneer of modernization who was imprisoned for almost 6 years (January 1899–August 1904), accused of advocating the institutionalization of a constitutional monarchy. He was a scholar who received a doctorate in international politics and law from Princeton University in 1910; an independence movement activist and first president of the Provisional Government of the Republic of Korea (1919–1948); and one of the most senior political leaders who became president of Korea at the age of 73, in a society where the political culture considered seniority to be important (Kim 2006, 63–68; Lee 2008; the *Joongang Ilbo*, June 14, 2010, 27).

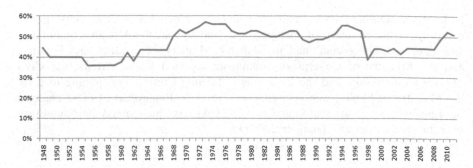

Fig. 2.6 Proportion of core executive apparatuses to total administrative apparatuses within the executive branch, 1948–2011

Considering that the institutionalization of the PS was weak, President Rhee's overall executive leadership can be said to have been effective, at least during the first half of his term, and can be explained partly by the large differentiation of the CAs during this period. Amidst this stage of state building, the administrative resources were extremely poor because of the near total destruction of this impoverished postcolonial country during the Korean War (1950–1953). Even under these circumstances, the Rhee administration invested a considerable amount of resources to institutionalize the CAs, which occupied 35 % or more of the total administrative apparatuses (Jung et al. 2011).

President Rhee's able executive leadership during his first term can be explained by his strong political coalitions with the administrative bureaucracy. Despite his charisma and political legitimacy, President Rhee—who spent much time abroad in exile—did not have a durable foundation in party politics in Korea. Thus, he preferred to communicate directly with the public rather than through a political party or the national assembly, and to cultivate political solidarity with the bureaucrats. Most of these bureaucrats had served during Japanese colonial rule and, therefore, lacked political legitimacy. They wanted to consolidate with President Rhee to overcome the issue of weak legitimacy and have their status protected. Against this backdrop, President Rhee was able to secure the loyalty of the bureaucrats and exert executive leadership effectively (Jung 2004).

Toward the second half of his term, President Rhee's abilities began to wane due to age and he became increasingly caught up with the bureaucracy. In a situation where a merit-based public personnel system was not institutionalized, the bureaucracy's neutral competence could hardly be improved. Besides, the governing Liberal Party founded by President Rhee had a low degree of democratic responsiveness (Lee 1968, 396). The political solidarity of Liberal Party politicians, who lacked democratic responsiveness, and the extremely politicized bureaucrats, brought about an abundance of injustice and corruption, leading to the administration being called the "Republic of Corruption" (Jung 2005).

The low level of democratic responsiveness, neutral competence, and executive leadership during the latter part of President Rhee's government made it difficult to efficiently pursue the national task of post-war reconstruction, not to mention long-term economic development planning and implementation. The Rhee administration collapsed after 12 years in power, due to a rigged presidential election in his third term, following the "April 19 Students' Uprising".

After the fall of President Rhee in April 1960, the Korean government amended the constitution and formed a parliamentary political executive. A large number of Koreans at that time regarded the presidential executive system as one of the main reasons that made the Rhee administration undemocratic. However, in less than a year, the experiment with a parliamentary executive system (from August 1960 to May 1961) proved ineffective as well. This failure was caused by several factors, one of which was the people's enthusiastic political participation after being suppressed by previous authoritarian governments, and the resultant sociopolitical conflicts and disintegration.

Also, Prime Minister Myon Chang's personal appeal and leadership were too weak to overcome the situation, even where there was no symbolic figure, such as a monarch, who was respected largely by the people and could contribute to forming a centripetal force in parliament and society. To make things worse, the institutionalization of either the PM's office or the CAs was too inadequate for the idealistic democratic leader to take control over the existing state bureaucracy (Figs. 2.4 and 2.6). In the end, Prime Minister Chang was overthrown after 10 months in power by a coup d'état led by the army—one of the state apparatuses that he was supposed to control in exercising his executive leadership.

2.3.2 Active Institutionalization of the Core Executive: Late 1960s to Late 1980s

During the second stage, the core executive was aggressively institutionalized to maximize the president's executive leadership (Fig. 2.6). General Chung-hee Park, who assumed power on May 16, 1961 through a military coup, amended the constitution to restore the presidential executive system. He was inaugurated in December 1963, after an election based on the new constitution, and began to actively pursue government-led industrialization. To achieve this, he initiated a great deal of reorganization, differentiating between economic and industrial policy apparatuses and strengthening the CAs and the PS (Fig. 2.1). Unlike his predecessors, President Park was well aware of the usefulness of staff organizations through his long experience as a military commander (Ham 1999; 2006).

Many bright, young people began to be employed in public posts in the early 1970s through a higher civil service examination and other open competitions. The merit-based career civil service, which has been institutionalized since the late 1960s, contributed to substantially improving the neutral competence of the administrative bureaucracy (Jung 2010). From this period on, the administrative bureaucracy began to keep its distance from interest groups, political parties, and even the national assembly, and was less prone to influence. President Park

(1961–1979) and his successor, Doo-hwan Chun (1980–1988), also prohibited bureaucrats from being affected by these groups, political parties, or the national assembly. Both presidents made use of the intricately institutionalized core executive apparatuses to control the administrative bureaucracy in a top-down manner.

President Park and the administrative bureaucrats shared the belief that the state administration should lead national development to catch up with industrialized countries. He was generous toward the bureaucrats, even those who had committed policy errors, so long as they pursued public policies consistent with his directions or value orientations. This brought him the bureaucrats' loyalty and obedience.

While Presidents Park and Chun and the administrative bureaucrats formed a strong nexus, neither president was wholly responsive to democratic accountability. In particular, 15 years from 1972 to 1987 saw representative democracy regress to an inordinate extent in Korea (Jung and Kim 2007). The link between the presidents' top-down executive leadership and the bureaucrats' neutral competence performed well in national development, simplified mainly as economic growth. Along with the regression of representative democracy, the government's responsiveness to public values other than economic growth was very weak. This regression, together with rapid industrialization, seemed to reject the "modernization thesis" and confirm the "bureaucratic authoritarianism" hypothesis in Korea (Jung and Kim 2007). With poor democratic responsiveness due to an increasingly "imperial presidency," the Korean people fiercely pursued the democratization movement, resulting in the demise of the Park administration in 1979 and the Chun administration in 1987.

2.3.3 The Dilemmatic Institutionalization of the Core Executive: Late 1980s to Present

For 25 years after the democratic transition in 1987, Korea has consolidated by passing the "two turn-over test" (Huntington 1991), first in 1997 and then in 2007. When the country's development is evaluated using a longer time span (i.e., from the 1960s to the 2000s), it can be considered a case that backs up the theory of "modernization," that is, by democratizing after being industrialized (Jung and Kim 2007). Since the democratic transition, there have been interesting changes in the executive leadership as well.

Most of all, people's negative sentiments began to spread concerning the predominance of the core executive, which was institutionalized during the authoritarian era. As a result, the presidents who took office after the democratic transition were pressured to reduce the size and role of the core executive apparatuses. Since the transition, therefore, the overall proportion of core executive apparatuses within the executive branch was reduced (Fig. 2.6). But this reduction was brought about by structural adjustments, not to the PS, but to the CAs, some of which were integrated with line ministries, as indicated above (Sect. 2.2.3)

Under the unfavorable circumstances regarding the dominance of the core executive, the presidents—especially those who needed legitimacy to conduct "small government" reforms—attempted to reduce the size or role of the PS, or used some symbolic gesture to suggest their intention of doing so, at least at the beginning of their term. But, as the PS began to grow again in the second half of their tenure, it resulted in the overall maintenance or even increase of the PS since the democratic transition (Fig. 2.1).

This may have been caused by the unrelenting pressure on each of the presidents to effectively achieve policy promises within their single 5-year term, stipulated in the constitution whose amendment had brought about the democratic transition of 1987. The stronger the determination of the presidents to fulfill their promises, the more they felt the need to control the bureaucracy, and hence rely more on the core executive apparatuses, especially the PS.

As such, successive Korean presidents have been faced with a dilemma during the past 25 years. On one hand, they have attempted to reduce and decentralize the PS to pursue further democratization and decentralization as well as a policy of "small government." On the other, they have had to rely on the more active role of the core executive apparatuses to fully implement public policies that they had pledged on the platform to win the presidential election.

Since 1987, there has also been a notable change in mutual confidence between presidents and administrative bureaucrats. Since then, the government party has alternated twice, with five new presidents assuming office every 5 years. In the process, the mutual confidence between presidents and bureaucrats has substantially declined. A newly inaugurated president, especially one who had brought in a change of government party, was less inclined to trust bureaucrats who had worked actively for the previous administration. As for the bureaucrats, they tended to be concerned that if they worked too hard for the current president, they would alienate themselves from the succeeding one. The more the mutual trust between the president and the bureaucrats has declined, the more the solidarity that formed between them during the authoritarian era has diminished, resulting in an increasingly complacent and indifferent attitude or behavior among bureaucrats toward the chief executive.

Despite changes in the mutual confidence between the president and the bureaucracy, the neutral competence of the latter has improved steadily. Civil servants have been provided with more diverse training opportunities both at home and abroad, and with more abundant policy knowledge that has been accumulated over the past six decades. Also, they have benefited in terms of status security by the strengthening of the merit-based career civil service during the decade following the democratic transition in 1987 (Jung 2010).

When the liquidity crisis affected Korea in 1997, the government began to conduct administrative reforms by actively adopting New Public Management (NPM) as suggested by the International Monetary Fund (Jung 2010). NPM reforms have had two significant outcomes in regard to executive leadership. The president has gained more opportunity to exercise control over the existing bureaucracy through these reforms, which challenge the guaranteed status of career civil servants by adopting an "open competition, contract-based, and performance-oriented" system of personnel management. While NPM reforms have provided the presidents with an opportunity to increase their capacity to control the bureaucracy more easily, they have also weakened the cohesion between the president and the bureaucracy. The newly adopted personnel management system—including the open competition, contract-based, and performance-oriented system and a Senior Executive Service—has brought about some confusion and deconstruction of the conventional administrative culture and institutions of integrity, cohesion, continuity, stability, and predictability based on hierarchical authority within the executive branch. The consequence has been a weakening of solidarity between presidents and bureaucrats.

Besides human resource management, the structural changes in administrative organizations have also worked as a factor in weakening the presidential executive leadership. Following the democratic transition, numerous social policy apparatuses were created to meet public service demands. In addition, many "parallel organizations"—mainly committees—were established to respond to the public mistrust of existing administrative apparatuses that actively served during the country's authoritarian rule. As a result, there was a rise in "organizational pluralism" (Rosenbloom 1993, 167–186), with increased checks and balances between administrative apparatuses (Jung 2010). This growth in organizational pluralism has lowered the president's capacity to coordinate policies and control the administrative bureaucracy. Since the democratic transition, successive presidents have had to face escalating conflicts not only among social groups due to an expansion in political participation, but also among administrative apparatuses within the executive branch on policy initiatives.

During the past 25 years, the government's democratic representativeness and responsiveness have been tremendously enhanced. The neutral competence of the administrative bureaucracy has also been greatly improved. However, the effectiveness of the president's executive leadership has declined in the increasingly complex environment.

2.4 Conclusion

The analyses in this chapter of the evolution of Korea's institutional presidency over the past six decades or so show some characteristics of institutional change and continuity in three different stages. The first stage was from the late 1940s to the early 1960s, when institutionalization of the PS was weak and the president depended mainly on his personal charisma and leadership capacity, along with the support of the highly expanded CAs, compared to the total administrative apparatuses. The second stage was from the late 1960s to the late 1980s, when a powerful core executive was institutionalized by differentiating the intraorganizational configurations of both the PS and the CAs according to public policy areas. And the third stage was from the late 1980s to the present, when presidents confronted

Table 2.2 Personnel backgrounds of core executive apparatuses in Korea, 1948–2011

		Career public servants	Politicians	Outside experts	Total
Presidential secretariat		180 (54.5 %)	42 (12.7 %)	108 (32.7 %)	330 (100 %)
Prime minister's office		66 (68.0 %)	17 (17.5 %)	14 (14.4 %)	97 (100 %)
Central agencies	Total	355 (67.2 %)	91 (17.2 %)	82 (15.5 %)	528 (100 %)
	Head	210 (60.3 %)	67 (19.3 %)	71 (20.4 %)	348 (100 %)
	Deputy head	145 (80.6 %)	24 (13.3 %)	11 (6.1 %)	180 (100 %)
Total		601 (62.9 %)	150 (15.7 %)	204 (21.4 %)	955 (100 %)

Note Units are persons. "Public servants" are career civil servants, military personnel, and judicial bureaucrats; "politicians" are members of political parties, the national assembly, and local councils and chief executives; "outside experts" are university professors, businessmen, bankers, journalists, and so on
Source Based on raw data from the National Archive (http://www.archives.go.kr/)

the dilemma of having to reduce the core executive to a decentralized, small and democratic government, and at the same time to enhance executive leadership capacity to effectively achieve their policy pledges.

As Fig. 2.6 shows, the core executive was expanded mostly during the period of rapid industrialization. From the late 1960s to the early 1990s, the proportion of core executive apparatuses to the total administrative apparatuses at the ministry level was at its highest. This was the period when Korea was governed by a conservative party. However, the proportion of core executive apparatuses was relatively low during the period when the country was governed by a liberal party (1960–1961 and 1998–2008). Even after the democratic transition in 1987, a top-down control mechanism of the executive leadership was maintained by concentrating decision-making largely in the hands of the president, with the intermediations of the PS and CAs within the executive branch.

The core executive apparatuses in Korea have been staffed largely with experts from within and outside the executive branch, rather than with politicians. During the past 60 years, nearly 63 % of the total staff in positions higher than vice ministers in the core executive apparatuses have been public servants; 21 % have been outside experts; while only 16 % have been politicians (Table 2.2).[3] This composition of personnel in the core executive has allowed its policies to be guided by the perspectives of "inside" public servants and "outside" experts, rather than politicians either from political parties or the national assembly, hence orienting it toward consistency and the longer term rather than flexibility and the shorter term.

Based on this analysis, a future direction for executive leadership development in the post-democratization period can be as follows: first, it is desirable to leave civil society with greater opportunities to define and resolve public problems by

---

[3] The only exception has been the short-lived Myon Chang government under the parliamentary executive system, when about 70 % of core executive positions were filled with politicians, while none was staffed by outside experts.

itself. Second, even in cases where the state may still need to resolve problems directly, more decentralization of policy functions and power would need to be pursued actively so that public policy problems would be solved at a local level by applying the subsidiarity principle. Third, it is necessary to decentralize decision-making power within the executive branch, delegating policy coordination from the core executive to administrative apparatuses, accompanied by effective performance evaluation and increased checks and balances among them.

References

Aberbach, J. D. (1990). *Keeping a watchful eye: the politics of congressional oversight.* Washington, DC: Brookings Institution.

Board of Audit and Inspection. (2008). *60-year history of the Board of Audit and Inspection of Korea.* Seoul: Board of Audit and Inspection.

Burke, J. P. (1992). *The institutional presidency.* Baltimore: The Johns Hopkins University Press.

Campbell, C., & Szablowski, G. J. (1979). *The superbureaucrats: structure and behavior in central agencies.* Toronto: MacMillan of Canada.

Cho, S. J., & Im, T. B. (2010). *Organization theory of Korean public administration (in Korean).* Pajoo: Bobmoonsa.

Chung, C. K. (1994). *Economic leadership of the presidents of Korea (in Korean).* Seoul: Korea Economic Daily.

Dickinson, M. J. (1997). *Bitter harvest: FDR, presidential power and the growth of the presidential branch.* New York: Cambridge University Press.

Dunleavy, P., & Rhodes, R. A. W. (1990). Core executive studies in Britain. *Public Administration, 68*(1), 3–28.

Finer, H. (1941). Administrative responsibility in democratic government. *Public Administration Review, 1*(4), 335–350.

Goodsell, C. T. (2004). *The case for bureaucracy: a public administration polemic* (4th ed.). Washington, DC: Congressional Quarterly Press.

Ham, S. D. (1999). *The Korean presidency (in Korean).* Pajoo: Nanam.

Han, S. (2010). Political resources and prime minister of partaker (in Korean). Unpublished doctoral dissertation, Seoul National University.

Heclo, H. (1975). OMB and the presidency—the problem of "neutral competence". *The Public Interest, 38*(Winter), 80–98.

Hobbes, T. (1651). *Leviathan.* Edited with an Introduction by C.B. Macpherson, Harmondsworth: Penguin Classics, 1981.

Huntington, S.P. (1991). *The third wave: democratization in the late twentieth century.* Norman: University of Oklahoma Press.

Johnson, C. (1982). *MITI and the Japanese miracle: the growth of industrial policy, 1925–1975.* Stanford: Stanford University Press.

Jung, Y.-D. (1996). Reforming the administrative apparatus in Korea: the case of the "civilian government". *International Review of Public Administration, 1*(1), 253–290.

Jung, Y.-D. (2004). The bureaucracy of the first republic of Korea. In J. Moon & S. Kim (Eds.), *Korean history in the 1950s (in Korean)* (pp. 127–164). Seoul: Sunin.

Jung, Y.-D. (2005). Stateness in transition: the Korean case in a comparative perspective. *Zeitschrift für Staats- und Europawissenschaften, 3*(3), 410–433.

Jung, Y.-D. (2007). The challenges of public administration reforms in Japan and South Korea. In D. Argyriades, O.P. Dwivedi, J.G. Jabbra (Eds.), *Public administration in transition: a fifty-year trajectory worldwide. Essays in honor of Gerald E. Caiden* (pp. 119–141). London: Vallentine Mitchell.

Jung, Y.-D. (2010). Change and continuity of the civil service system in Korea. Keynote speech at the international conference on the occasion of the 80th anniversary of the Examination Yuan of the Republic of China, Taipei.

Jung, Y.-D., & Kim, C. (2007). The institutionalisation of representative democracy in Korea, 1948–2007. In F. Grotz & T.A.J. Toonen (Eds.), *Crosing borders: constitutional development and internationalisation. Essays in honour of Joachim Jens Hesse* (pp. 136–152). Berlin: De Gruyter Recht.

Jung, Y.-D., Kwon, Y., Kim, G. (2002) *A function analysis of the office of government policy coordination*. Research report. Korean Political Science Association, Seoul, December 2002.

Jung, Y.-D., Lee, Y.-H., & Kim, D.-S. (2011). Institutional change and continuity in Korea's central agencies, 1948–2011. *Korean Journal of Policy Studies, 26*(1), 21–48.

Jung, Y.-D., Yoo, H.-J., Lee, Y.-H. (2010). The executive leadership in South Korea, 1948–2010: from charismatic to institutional presidency. Paper presented to Working Group VII on Leadership, Governance and Public Policy at the 28th international congress of administrative sciences. International Institute of Administrative Sciences and the International Association of Schools and Institutes of Administration, Bali.

Jung, Y.-D. (2012). The evolution of institutional presidency in Korea, 1948–2011. *Japanese Review of Political Society, 1*(1), 27–44.

Kaufman, H. (1956). Emerging conflicts in the doctrines of public administration. *American Political Science Review, 50*(December), 1057–1073.

Kim, C.-N. (2006). *Leadership for nation-building: Korean Presidents from Syngman Rhee to Kim Dae-jung (in Korean)*. Seoul: Seoul National University Press.

Lee, H.-B. (1968). *Korea: time, change and administration*. Honolulu: East-West Center Press.

Lee, J. Y. (2008). *Woonam Syngman Rhee, who is he?*. Seoul: Pai Chai Academy.

Locke, J. (1689). *Two treatises of government*. Edited by P. Laslett, Cambridge: Cambridge University Press, 1960.

Meier, K. J. (1997). Bureaucracy and democracy: the case for more bureaucracy and less democracy. *Public Administration Review, 57*(3), 193–199.

Moe, T. M. (1993). Presidents, institutions, and theory. In G. C. Edwards, J. H. Kessel, & B. A. Rockman (Eds.), *Researching the presidency: vital questions, new approaches* (pp. 337–386). Pittsburgh: University of Pittsburgh Press.

Ministry of Government Administration and Home Affairs. (1998). *A history of Korean government organizations (in Korean)*. Seoul: Ministry of Government Administration and Home Affairs.

Peters, B.G., Rhodes, R.A.W., Wright, V. (Eds.) (2000). *Administering the summit: administration of the core executive in developed countries*. New York: Palgrave Macmillan.

Rockman, B. A. (1984). Legislative-executive relations and legislative oversight. *Legislative Studies Quarterly, 9*(3), 387–440.

Rose, R. (1984). *The capacity of the president: a comparative analysis*. Studies in Public Policy No. 130. Glasgow: University of Strathclyde.

Rosenbloom, D. (1993). *Public administration* (3rd ed.). New York: MacGraw-Hill.

Yoo, H.-J., & Lee, Y.-H. (2010). Historical analysis on the development of an institutional presidency. *Korean Public Administration Review, 44*(2), 111–136.

Chapter 3
Managing Economic Policy and Coordination: A Saga of the Economic Planning Board

Byung-Sun Choi

3.1 Introduction

It is hard to imagine the successful economic development of South Korea without the Economic Planning Board (EPB).[1] Created in 1961 when Korea embarked on its long-term economic development planning, the EPB, which occupied the center of the country's economic policymaking and coordination structure, was in existence for 33 years before being suddenly dissolved in 1994. Korea's economic policymaking and coordination structure and process have since drifted. With all the intermittent attempts to revive it in one form or another, the problem of ineffective and inefficient coordination of economic policy has surfaced time and again. This chapter seeks to unfold the saga of the EPB with a view to drawing out implications for developing countries that are struggling to build up organizational capacities to handle a diverse set of developmental tasks and problems.

Discussion and analysis in this chapter will center on answering the following question: What made the EPB so unique and special and, as a result, hard to replicate once it was gone? To answer this question, the chapter will focus on the sources of the EPB's institutional strengths. Particular emphasis will be placed on pointing out and correcting two seemingly widely shared misunderstandings about the sources of the EPB's power and influence. For one, the fact that the EPB had planning as well as budgeting functions tended to lead to the belief that putting these two functions together in the same organization would guarantee an effective and efficient implementation of economic development plans. It was not necessarily so. Instead, this chapter argues that what is important is not simply to link these

---

[1] See Mason et al. (1980), Jones and Sakong (1980) and Kim et al. (1987).

B.-S. Choi (✉)
Graduate School of Public Administration, Seoul National University, Seoul 151-742,
Republic of Korea
e-mail: bschoi1@snu.ac.kr

H. Kwon and M. G. Koo (eds.), *The Korean Government and Public Policies*
in a Development Nexus, Volume 1, The Political Economy of the Asia Pacific,
DOI: 10.1007/978-3-319-01098-4_3, © Springer International Publishing Switzerland 2014

two functions as closely and tightly as possible, but to make each an effective but related instrument of policy coordination, the necessity of which would constantly arise in the process of following-up on development plans. The reason behind this argument is that effective and competent economic policymaking and coordination are more important, when the need arises, than economic development plans themselves. This is especially so in light of the fact that it is often only at the follow-up stage that new bottlenecks, obstacles, problems, or new investment opportunities and so forth that were not anticipated either fully or in part at the planning stage, can be dealt with properly and more wisely.

The argument that Hirschman made in the 1950s is particularly apt here: "[in underdeveloped countries, especially,] the role of government must frequently be viewed as 'induced' rather than 'inducing.'"[2] What this means is that to the extent that economic development plans cannot be made complete, especially for reasons of insufficient information,[3] It is essential for the government to resolve effectively and efficiently the problems, bottlenecks, shortages, and so on that may arise necessarily and naturally in the course of implementing the plans. It is often through this sequential process that the government is most able to identify current pressing issues—new problems, or new opportunities that were unforeseen or unexpected at the time of planning—and act in the most informed manner possible. In this sense, while it is necessary to draw up comprehensive development plans well, it is conceivably more important to respond effectively to any unanticipated developments through successful policy coordination. After all, this perhaps is what coordination is all about.[4]

Viewed from this perspective, the factor that made the EPB so unique and special in performing its mission was not simply the putting together of planning and budgeting functions in one organization, but the exploitation of its institutional strengths. This gave the EPB a privileged place in the structure of economic policymaking and coordination and permitted it to play a central role. The author argues that it was the institutional autonomy of the EPB that made it unique and led it to possess a broad and long-term perspective, and enjoy a high degree of

---

[2] Hirschman (1958: 203).

[3] Plans can be—and usually are—revised intermittently. But this fact is irrelevant, at least for the present discussion, since even in these cases there still remains the need to adapt or adjust them to the constantly changing economic conditions and situations.

[4] By its own nature, economic policy coordination tends not only to be complex and conflict-ridden, but tedious and cumbersome as well. It is especially true for developing countries since they are, as a rule, confronted with innumerable developmental needs, but lack economic resources and other prerequisites for development. This is not meant to imply that the advanced and fully democratized countries do not need an effective economic policy coordination structure and process any more. It may, arguably, be more necessary for these latter countries because their societies tend to be highly plural, and democratic politics tends to make the process of coordination more difficult and complex. What is stressed here is simply that, in developing countries, setting up priority through effective coordination in the early period of economic development is a critically important factor in determining the course of development. In advanced countries, by contrast, it tends to be relegated to a matter of effective, or less effective, political accommodation.

flexibility in making economic policy choices. This turned out to be instrumental in steering the course of economic development in the direction deemed most desirable, in the face of turns and twists of economic and political developments both within the country and outside.[5]

Another facet of the EPB that has often been overlooked is the reason why, and how, it could secure such strong political support from the country's presidents, which may constitute a sufficient reason for its ability to play so effective a role as the proximate central coordinator. A seemingly conventional belief is that it was simply because the special status of deputy prime minister (DPM) had been conferred on the minister of the EPB. It may be true, but only partly so. The rationale against this belief is that it may be a necessary condition, but not a sufficient one, because the conferring of this status alone cannot guarantee the trust and confidence of a president. The author's argument is that the political support of the president was something that the EPB had to earn strenuously in a never-ending policy competition among related ministries through the adroit and strategic management of its political mandate, and through an extraordinary effort to build up its own unique organizational capabilities and competencies.

3.2 A Brief History of the EPB

Korea's system of economic policymaking and coordination, and its core mechanisms and processes, have undergone some significant changes, in step with the changing stages of economic and political development. Nonetheless, the economic policy management style, formed gradually in the 1960s, has been embedded so firmly in the structure of economic policy management that, despite a succession of government restructuring afterward, the essential characteristics still remain. At the heart of the country's economic policy management, at least for the period of the EPB's existence, was the "central" coordination by the DPM.[6] Except for some symbolic value, the status of the DPM had no constitutional basis or legal force, signifying that the EPB was a sort of head ministry having formal authority to coordinate economic policy overall. This unique setup worked perfectly well during President Park's rule and reasonably well under the two ex-military presidents after him. The real challenge against the EPB started with the

---

[5] As will be shown in this chapter, the EPB's policy flexibility did not always work in the interest of the EPB, since it tended to inhibit it from building political support for its organization, as was evidenced by the continued wrangle over its fate that led eventually to its demise in 1994.

[6] The meaning of central coordination needs some clarification. Central coordination is defined here as follows: among a set of decision-makers, coordination is central to the degree that there is in the set one decision-maker who (a) is much more powerful than the others, and (b) explicitly recognizes his task to be that of arranging the adaptation of decisions one to another and, to some significant degree, arranges such adaptations. This definition is borrowed from Lindblom (1965: 103–105).

coming of the so-called "civilian" democratic governments in the 1990s, although a variety of criticisms had been leveled against the EPB from time to time. Ironically enough, most of the criticisms were made not because the EPB failed to perform its mission, but because it performed its mission only too well, as will be analyzed in the subsequent sections.

The EPB was created in July 1961, 2 months after the military coup led by Park Chung-hee. Its establishment was meant to symbolize the military government's strong commitment to economic development and, as a necessary corollary to it, a systematic and sustained pursuit of long-term economic development planning as well.[7] The EPB took over the functions of comprehensive development planning and foreign cooperation from the Ministry of Construction, which had been established only a month earlier by the same military junta.[8] It also absorbed the Bureau of Budget from the Ministry of Finance (MOF) and the Bureau of Statistics from the Ministry of Home Affairs to ensure the effective and efficient execution of development programs and to support the drawing up of comprehensive plans. Although the EPB was formally equipped both with planning and budget functions, and had some indirect control over financial policy and the allocation of foreign aid and loans, it had to frequently fight against inflation caused mainly by over ambitious public investment programs. Repeated failures taught a lesson to the EPB that it needed further strengthening of its mandate to be able to coordinate economic

---

[7] Economic planning in Korea began well before the military coup in 1961. The initial effort at economic planning was started during the Korean War by foreign assistance agencies. But the program, prepared by Robert R. Nathan Associates and known as the Nathan plan, was never formally adopted or even recognized by the Korean government. In 1959, the Syngman Rhee government developed a seven-year plan. The first phase of this program was formulated and approved by the cabinet in January, 3 months before President Rhee was overthrown. A new five-year plan (1962–1966), prepared by the cabinet of Prime Minister Chang Myon in 1961, was shelved due to the military coup in May that year. For a detailed account of planning in Korea, see Cole and Nam (1969).

[8] From the start, the idea of turning the Ministry of Reconstruction (1955–1961), which had a modest planning function, into the EPB, which would have both planning and budgeting functions, was proposed to the military junta by a few reform-minded officials. But the military coup leader, Park Chung-hee, decided to turn it first into the Ministry of Construction and then to the EPB. The reasones for his decision to follow this schematic approach still remain unclear. But the scanty evidence tells us that by turning it into the Ministry of Construction, General Park wanted to symbolize to the public his full commitment and devotion to the "economy-first policy." The public was unsure of the legitimacy of the sudden military coup that had overthrown the democratic government which had been legitimately instituted only a year before, following the April 19 Student Revolution. Also, General Park himself was uncertain of the fate of the military coup. He felt it was too premature and bold to go forward with the establishment of the EPB and launch full-scale planning efforts while the prospect of continued foreign aid flows remained bleak due to the reluctance of donating countries to recognize the coup. This economic policy concern was the reason for giving the Ministry of Construction its English-language name, the Ministry of Development, which was thought to be instrumental in keeping up the inflow of foreign aid, given the fact that foreign aid was necessarily tied to reconstruction and development projects. See Kim (1999: 23–74).

and industrial policy more effectively. Under these circumstances, and especially pressed by the EPB, President Park decided to confer on the minister of the EPB the newly created status of DPM in December 1963.

With hindsight, that decision was a watershed in the building of a new working relationship among government ministries. The elevation of its status did not necessarily mean that the other ministries were to be subjected constitutionally or legally to the EPB's—or, for that matter, the DPM's—direction and coordination. But by presidential decree, other ministers, regardless of whether their ministries were economic or not, were required to have prior consultations with the DPM when they wished to initiate major policy proposals. With this preclearance procedure in place, two disparate tendencies evolved over time. First, the regular meetings of economic ministers presided over by the DPM proliferated, and the DPM began to assume the role of the government's economic policy team leader. Second, by contrast, the noneconomic ministers tended to skip the prior consultation process and, as a result, inter-ministerial conflicts over policy initiatives arose from time to time. This was particularly true of the noneconomic ministries, such as the ministries of foreign, defense, and home affairs, among others. It was not only because their policy proposals did not involve unusual budget expenditures, but because the case of their policy proposals tended to rest on noneconomic grounds.[9]

Nevertheless, as time went on, the EPB began to evolve as a center of economic policymaking and coordination, with the DPM as economic policy team leader and the government's principal economic policy spokesman. What perhaps needs emphasizing more than anything else is that the EPB, created later than other economic ministries, came quickly to hold the center stage in providing coherence to a diverse set of economic development plans and programs. Conventional wisdom appears to hold that the EPB's successful performance was made possible only because it was equipped with planning and budgeting authority and functions—two powerful policy instruments. This was the main motive of the reform-minded officials who had proposed the establishment of the EPB, and it was also the motive that persuaded the military junta led by President Park. However, this is a vast oversimplification. Although holding these instruments may have been a necessary condition for the EPB to wield power and influence over other ministries, it was certainly not sufficient for it to have accomplished its mission well. To get down to the very secret of the EPB's extraordinary achievement, one needs to look more deeply into the mode and style of management of economic policymaking and coordination in Korea. To this end, the next section examines the institutional characteristics of the EPB and the reasons that enabled it to win the strong political support of the country's presidents.

---

[9] This does not necessarily mean that the economic ministries had no policy conflict with the EPB. In many instances, the more hotly and intensely fought battles were mainly between them and the EPB.

3.3 The Sources of the EPB's Institutional Preeminence

3.3.1 State/Society Linkages and Institutional Autonomy

The first thing to note is the big difference in state/society linkages between the EPB and other economic ministries, which affected the relative strength and position of each in the workings of policy competition among them.[10] Unlike other ministries, the EPB had no particular constituents or client groups in society that made strong demands or put enormous pressure to take on a particular policy direction in their favor. This institutional characteristic presented the EPB with a high degree of autonomy and flexibility in choosing among economic policies and making policy judgments, while other ministries were forced to find themselves constrained in their policy choices. The institutional autonomy of the EPB uniquely offered it an image that the policy positions it took would surely reflect the realities of the economy more correctly, and thus represent common rather than special interests. The EPB's institutional autonomy also acted as a spur to look to the longer term rather than the pressures of the moment. As a result, policy reversal was a sort of norm for the EPB whenever it deemed it desirable and necessary, which however was a source of animosity from the perspective of other ministries.

Probably the most laudable achievement of the EPB in the long process of Korean economic development may be the stable management of the economy. Without institutional autonomy and its resultant policy flexibility, along with broad and long-term perspectives, the EPB could not have played that role so superbly. When it perceived inflationary pressures mounting in the economy, for instance, it did not hesitate to alter the course of economic policy in the direction of slowdown. When the economy was in a deflationary mood, it took the initiative to steer the economy in the opposite direction, for example, by launching investment programs earlier than scheduled.[11] This role of keeping the economy well on track could not have been played effectively if the EPB had insufficient autonomy and had to pander to short-term and parochial interests. Of course, if the DPM and EPB lacked the president's firm confidence, the EPB may have failed to play this role at all in the first place, another interesting issue that will be discussed in the following section.

Still another—and probably more important—factor that helped the EPB play its role so effectively was a keenly felt need for organizational competence. The authority and responsibility given to the DPM and EPB to lead the pack of economic ministries, coordinate economic policies, and mediate and resolve disputes among frequently antagonistic government departments, pressed the EPB hard to

---

[10] The idea originated from the author's 1987 doctoral dissertation on *Institutionalizing A Liberal Economic Order in Korea: The Strategic Management of Economic Change*.

[11] To put it differently, the commitment cost to be borne by the EPB was almost always less than that of other economic ministries.

acquire organizational competence quickly, given the fact that the task of maintaining a minimum level of coherence and consistency in government actions proved inherently difficult. Moreover, carrying out the mission and the responsibility to mediate between contending interests, and imposing a measure of discipline on pluralistic politics, turned out to be even more demanding. The question then is: What did the EPB do to strengthen its organizational competence?

The institutional autonomy of the EPB comes into play here again. It not only constituted the EPB's fundamental source of influence and authority, but also led it—independently and creatively—to develop its own organizational competence. Given its unique status, the EPB had no interest groups or organizations to look to or rely on for information and analysis. As a result, it needed to foster analytical capability and expertise of its own to perform its mission competently. Because it's main tasks were, in essence, to force—or at least facilitate—comparisons and trade-offs among competing and frequently conflicting policy proposals made by other ministries, the EPB felt a constant need to excel in policy competition among related ministries. What enabled the EPB to get the upper hand in this policy competition was invariably the fact that it was institutionally free from the particular demands and pressures of any group in society. This institutional autonomy, in turn, gave the EPB's policy analyses a high level of objectivity, and thus persuasiveness, and helped bring its broader and longer term perspectives to bear on the coordination process so forcefully.

The EPB, which started small, continued to grow and diversify organizationally in response to the rise in its analytical tasks.[12] It tried hard to staff the organization by recruiting widely for able people. What contributed more to developing its organizational capacity was an on-the-job training carried out ministry-wide. As most officials in the EPB were constantly confronted with the same or similar tasks, a nonhierarchical organizational culture emerged that valued free debate and communication, both among peers and between superiors and subordinates. It was not infrequently observed that officials, regardless of rank, would get together to discuss and debate for long hours until they reached some kind of consensus on the issues at hand. It was also not infrequent for the DPM to summon low-ranking officials—bypassing their direct superiors—who, in his opinion, possessed the most valuable information. This unusual practice further helped to bring down hierarchical barriers in the organization, while enhancing competition for excellence among cadres in the EPB. In short, the EPB had evolved in a brief period of time into a highly effective learning organization.

This organizational culture was of an unprecedented type and nature in the bureaucracy of Korea. In the previous government, for instance, the bureaucracy was largely corrupt and irresponsible in the face of constant political instability. It lacked both confidence in itself and the belief that it could initiate and lead the development process to bring the country out of poverty. With the advent of

---

[12] Certainly there was an economy of scale and scope for the organizational growth of the EPB. But it should be noted that it provided a cause for the frequent claims by other ministries that the EPB had become an overarching ministry and needed to be reformed.

military leaders onto the political scene, the bureaucracy was shaken to its roots, and the new view was that the EPB needed to become the foremost "agent of change." That "the government ought to be the agent of change" was a buzzword in the early 1960s, especially among reform-minded military leaders and government officials.[13] It is not an exaggeration that the reorganization of the government in the early 1960s was aimed primarily at producing that change.

Before closing this section, it would be helpful to compare the state/society linkages of the EPB with that of other ministries. In stark contrast to the EPB, many economic ministries in Korea had major groups in society as their clients: The Ministry of Commerce and Industry (MCI) served the interests of business; the Ministry of Agriculture and Fisheries the farm community; the Ministry of Labor the labor groups; and so on. The linkages of these ministries with their easily identifiable constituent groups were strong for two reasons. First, the absence or weakness of other linkages tended to reinforce the interdependent relationship between government agencies and their respective constituent groups. As a result, these ministries played a crucial role as intermediaries for the influence of major societal groups, such as the *chaebol*—or large business conglomerates—organized labor, and medium- and small-size enterprises. Even the *chaebol,* which the public believed politically powerful, had no other avenue to exert its influence without counting on the relevant government agencies. In other words, from the perspective of these interest groups, government agencies were nothing but an assured source of advocacy.

A second factor that strengthened this interrelationship was strategic: In the politicized market economy, a relatively small change in sector by sector policy, such as import protection measures, makes a big difference in consequences for the private, as opposed to social, profitability of many economic activities.[14] Therefore, client groups had to have a keen interest in keeping a good and close relationship with government agencies to protect their interests. On the government side, to the degree that their constituent industries embodied their institutional goals and visions of legitimate action, government agencies had every incentive to be responsive to their demands and to foster the health and growth of

---

[13] It is noteworthy that, around this time, it was the military and not the government that had gone through the Korean War and been exposed to the advanced administrative knowledge and skills handed down mostly from the United States military. Right after the coup, therefore, young military officers and reform-minded government officials exchanged ideas and worked closely to turn the government into an agent of change by giving each government agency a clear mission and objective and ensuring its performance by adopting an evaluation system. It is no surprise, then, that the government structure quite closely resembled a military organization. Using an analogy, the EPB acted like a military headquarters, run by competent staff, responsible for logistics, planning and strategy, and coordination and feedback. See Kim (1999: 23–74). Incidentally, it was also no accident that the Graduate School of Public Administration, Seoul National University—established in 1959 with the aid of the United Nations Development Programme—began to provide administrative knowledge to upgrade the country's bureaucracy.

[14] On this argument and its implications for patterns of mutual adjustment between the state and society in a politicized market economy, see Barzelay (1986: Chap. 4).

their constituents. This strong interrelationship almost always acted to make each individual government agency have a narrow policy preference and, as a result, its policy choices were constrained, which was never the case with the EPB.

The EPB, incidentally, tried hard to prevent any operating responsibilities—often taken on by other ministries as their core business—from being incorporated into the EPB. This was wise, as the responsibilities would have harmed the EPB's institutional autonomy which was crucial to accomplishing its integral tasks of coordinating economic and industrial policies from a broader and longer term perspective, and changing the direction of economic policy for the benefit of the economy as a whole. In brief, the institutional autonomy was the cornerstone on which the EPB could secure the authority and legitimacy it required so dearly to perform its tasks effectively and competently.

3.3.2 Strong Political Support for the DPM (and the EPB)

As mentioned in the preceding section, there is no doubt that the EPB's power and influence could not be exerted effectively unless it could enjoy the confidence and strong political support of the president. The question then is: Why did President Park put so much confidence in the DPM and the EPB? It must be made clear here that the president's trust was not so much in the people themselves—even if he selected the DPMs with extreme care—but in the institutional mission and capability embodied in the status and role of the DPM (and EPB).

Presidents always appear to face two genuine problems that are never resolved satisfactorily.[15] First, how could a presidential intervention be reconciled with an agency responsible for its own performance and striving for its independence? Second, could the president intervene without damaging his own record, in a way that would provide for effective implementation of his policies? How, above all, could an effective presidential intervention be assured without overburdening the president? In the case of Korea, at least, the experiment of establishing and operating an effective coordinating body seems to have offered a fairly satisfactory answer. By counting heavily on the DPM, and abstaining from intervening preemptively into the decision-making and coordination process led by the DPM, the president could show to the nation that he had a rein on the economic policy-making process through the DPM, while shielding himself from any political blame in case of policy failure.

To understand this policy management structure and style more fully, it would be helpful to review the usual process in which significant decisions were made under President Park. Being accustomed to the military, he preferred decisions being made on the spot. During his rule, it was customary that important decisions requiring government-wide cooperation and nationwide effort were made in such meetings as the "New Year's Ministry Report to the President," "Expanded

---

[15] Schick (1981: 108).

Meeting for Export Promotion," and "Implementation Report on the New Village Movement" (also known as *Saemaul Undong*) over which he presided. In these meetings, President Park heard reports, mostly from ministers concerned, on the analysis of past performance, the current situation and problems ahead. He would ask a few questions, invite comments from a few participants, and—as his final decision—sanction the future action plans as revised. In these meetings, the president invariably sought the opinion of the DPM, sending a signal that he regarded the DPM's consent as an absolute prerequisite for any plan to be finalized. What is notable is that the DPM rarely expressed dissent. There was little need to do so, since every major plan had already been cleared through the prior coordination process with the EPB. Insofar as the president made it a rule to solicit the opinion of the DPM, no minister dared say anything to the president as it was certain to be rebutted by the DPM in front of the president.

Among the many characteristic aspects of these meetings, what President Park seemed to value most highly was the openness and "constructive" criticism. He considered them an effective means to ensure cooperation among key players, both from government ministries and the private sector. As long as decisions were made by the president himself in front of all the participants—and mostly televized in their entirety or in part to the public—it was impossible for anyone not to deliver what was decided upon openly. President Park appreciated his image as a highly decisive man who could make decisions on the spot. It was a great opportunity and privilege, especially for those from the private sector, to make their grievances and complaints known to the president. Frequently, the complaints and appeals were addressed to the slower or less cooperative government agencies. It was only natural, then, for every minister and agency head to try and avoid unexpected public blame, which in turn helped generate far greater cooperative and concerted action among players than it otherwise would.

This style of decision-making at the top was the hallmark of President Park, indicating his managerial ingenuity. Most of all, he believed in, and committed himself to, the merit system in the civil service. Being a man of discipline, his strict application of this discipline seemed to be the single most important factor that got the latent bureaucracy to go about its work seriously, and big business leaders to go along with the government's wishes. President Park made it a principle to reward good performance and punish that which was bad, especially one that resulted from malfeasance or wrong intentions. If discipline constituted the backbone of his administrative philosophy, competition formed another major component in his managerial toolkit. He knew how to make the best use of rivalry and competition among his subordinates for the benefit of getting work done well. Whenever he was in doubt, for instance, he commissioned more than two—usually three—persons to conduct their individual analyses and report to him privately. In other cases, which were more frequent, he would arrange a meeting in which each person, who thought he was the only one charged, was asked to report his analysis and recommendations in front of his rivals. In these ways, the president elicited new information and prompted conflicting views and opinions on the state of affairs in question in an effort to reach a more objective and reasonable decision.

This managerial and decision-making style of the president fitted in well with the role that the DPM was expected to play. One might say that given such a president and the decision-making structure at the highest levels, the DPM's role could well have been superfluous. But, emphatically, it was not. The structure and style of decision-making at the top could not be thought of without the DPM and the EPB. The DPM's role and function, too, could not have been successfully executed if the president's decision-making style was any different. This fortunate coincidence should not blind one to the fact that the policy coordination structure and process in Korea—centering on the EPB—had something special that an effective coordination structure and process ought to possess.

It relates to the reasons why top decision-makers tend to place confidence in, and provide forceful political support for, effective coordinators such as the DPM (and the EPB) in the case of Korea. First, in order to realize his vision of modernizing the country, the central decision-maker needs somebody to mastermind the entire process competently in support of him. That "somebody," in the case of President Park, could only have been the DPM. President Park took power in a military coup, and the only cause that could legitimize his action was one that delivered the country from poverty and corruption. Also, since he lacked practical economic knowledge and managerial experience, at least in the civilian sector, he needed to find someone who was knowledgeable in economics and skillful and effective in getting things done. Second, as a result, the DPM was given a far wider scope of mission in fulfilling the president's "revolutionary" vision than any other economic minister.[16] This wider scope of mission of the DPM brought him closer to the president and political elites, with the result that the DPM could enjoy stronger political support than any other minister.

Third, in full consideration of these reasons, President Park took pains to select a DPM he could trust and count on heavily once selected. All the DPMs that President Park selected belonged to this category; they were honored in their respective fields for these qualities. To the extent that he painstakingly chose these men, there arose a tendency to organize the economic policy team with those who would work harmoniously with them.[17] And this tendency, in turn, engendered a new tradition in Korea to keep the DPM in his post for as long as possible to maintain the continuity and stability of economic policy while replacing other economic ministers more often. Along with this, yet another new tradition was being built into the system where the vice and assistant ministers of the EPB were routinely picked as heads of other economic ministries.[18]

---

[16] As a matter of fact, the leaders of the military coup called their takeover a revolution to rebuild the country from the root up, pulling it out of corruption and poverty.

[17] It is notable that President Park—and for that matter other presidents after him as well—rarely gave the DPM a voice in the assignment of economic ministers.

[18] This has a profound implication for the effectiveness of the coordination process, as other ministers, recruited from the EPB, were well versed in the process of economic planning and policy coordination.

The president's intention to build a team to oversee economic and industrial policy was also at work in his pattern of choosing an Economic Secretary to the President (ESP), another key player in Korea's economic policymaking and coordination structure.[19] Throughout his tenure, President Park consistently gave the ESP the status of vice minister while selecting him from among the upper echelons of the EPB or MOF or, in rare cases, from other economic ministries such as the MCI.[20] Quite obviously, this practice reflected the president's intention to keep the ESP subordinate—at least in terms of formal rank—to the DPM. Although the ESP was the closest advisor to him, the president wanted to make sure that the ESP did not dare risk tipping the balance he had consciously set up among the key economic policymakers.

As a result, any disagreement between the DPM and ESP was rarely made public and did not develop into political bickering or scandal. Instead, the differences—if any—were resolved quietly between them, or through the president's intervention. Whenever there was a difference in their opinions, and the president tended to take sides with him, the ESP acted as a messenger to let the DPM know the president's preference. In view of the president's wish that the economic policy team work in unison and produce concerted policy action, the ESP tended to communicate frequently with the DPM in an effort to strike out differences, if any, while he pressed other economic ministers to go along with the DPM. In this way, the ESP acted as the cement linking all key players and as a catalyst having them move together in the same direction. However, there were times in the history of the EPB in which this balance of power between the DPM and the ESP changed in the latter's favor, as illustrated in Sect. 4.5.

To sum up, it would be fair to say that the president's political support for the DPM remained strong and intact throughout President Park's tenure. The DPM's influence and performance as the economic policy team leader varied from one DPM to another, depending presumably on the ability, personal traits, and effectiveness of the DPM himself in taking advantage of his political mandate. But it still remains true that he, most of all, enjoyed the president's confidence and vigorous political support. To the degree that the president put great confidence in him—and it was well understood by other economic ministers as to who would generally prevail if a controversy reached the president for resolution—it was easy enough for the DPM to make his coordination results succeed, representing another important benefit of this economic policy coordination structure and style.

---

[19] The ESP had only a few staff members, so that it was difficult for him to get involved in program operations. As a result, the ESP acted more as a president's clerk, or sentinel and guardian, rather than a high official with his own power and independence. As will be shown later in this chapter, the ESPs subsequently tended to be advocates of a particular economic policy. For the differentiated roles of presidential advisors, see Porter (1980: 73–83).

[20] This tendency became pronounced from the early 1970s, when President Park had enough time to handpick capable men and further strengthen his grip on the bureaucracy.

3.4 The EPB's Strategic Management of Economic Policy Change: An Episode

Probably the most significant economic policy change that the EPB initiated and put into effect may be the one that took place between the late 1970s and early 1980s. It aimed at turning away fundamentally from the existing economic and industrial policy regime—which centered on developing heavy and chemical industries—in an effort to substitute imports and increase large-scale production capacities for export to a more market-oriented and open economy by liberalizing trade, the financial sector, and foreign exchange. This economic policy turnaround was attempted in the midst of rising inflation that went as far as to threaten the existing political order and stability.

Since its inception, the EPB had concerned itself with inflation brought on sporadically by massive government and private investment. Even though it influenced all sectors of the economy, inflation was not the concern of the other economic ministries. In identifying policy options and weighing their consequences, these ministries were far less concerned with the effects of their policy on other sectors of the economy. Problems posed by rising inflation in the late 1970s were of an extraordinary nature in that they had strong political significance. Despite rapid economic growth, the inflation then escalating went so far as to erode the tolerance of the people, who did not welcome or necessarily accept the new political regime and growing income inequality.[21] As Hirschman argued, during the first phase of the country's rapid economic growth, even those who were left behind felt encouraged and tended to support the existing order for a while in the hope that their turn would surely arrive. However, as that economic progress was perceived by the rest to be restricted to one distinct and closed group, political and social tension escalated.[22] Under these circumstances, the EPB began to advocate import liberalization and successfully managed the policy process to make its preference prevail. Why and how did the EPB do this?

In this politically precarious situation, President Park tended to stick to his belief that a continued and more rapid economic growth would sustain the legitimacy of his regime. Many other ministers—both economic and noneconomic—were, on one

---

[21] The *Yushin* (meaning "restoration") is the political regime that President Park instituted in 1972 to prolong his rule of the country under the pretext of securing it from a military threat from North Korea. On one hand, he amended the constitution, under which the president would be elected indirectly by an electoral college and all term limits would be removed. On the other, he promised the people that by 1978, when his first term in office under the new constitution would end, he would accomplish the dual goals of "national income $1,000, exports $10 billion." The development of heavy and chemical industries for automobiles, electronics, shipbuilding, petrochemicals, and so on—which were evaluated as economically non-viable by the World Bank, among others—constituted the core and integral part of the heavy and chemical industry drive. The *Yushin* regime met with vehement resistance, including from opposition parties, labor, and university student bodies.

[22] See Hirschman (1979: 63).

hand, encouraged by the president's strong commitment to sector by sector industrial policies, including heavy and chemical industries and many rural development projects. On the other, they were overtaken by parochial interests and reluctant to cut down any of the existing schemes or review the existing policy course critically,[23] as if inflation had been the problem for which the EPB alone was to be held responsible.[24] By contrast, the EPB recognized the immense political and social implications of inflation and had little reason to go on with expansive industrial policies that were seen as a fundamental cause of the inflation.[25] Given the seriousness of the difference in their policy views, it was inevitable that the struggle between other operating ministries and the EPB was drawing quickly to a head.

Under these circumstances, the strategy that the EPB used was to make inflation not just the EPB's problem alone but the president's too, and thus bring his influence to bear on other ministries reluctant to go along with the EPB. Accordingly, the EPB devised a policy argument especially palatable to the president himself. It stated that reducing the pace of the heavy and chemical industry drive—the economic policy nature of which was import-substituting—by ushering in a certain degree and element of import liberalization would not only help reduce inflationary pressures, but also provide a better environment later on for those industries and other sector by sector investment programs that the president had committed himself to. The EPB even sought to bring the influence of some of the other ministries' client groups that were being hurt by high inflation—such as the export industry group—to bear on those ministries in an effort to induce changes in their attitude toward the existing policy. Being always mindful of public opinion on the state of the economy, the EPB paid special attention to the press in an effort to arouse public opinion in support of its policy reversal. All these strategic actions, in effect, acted in part to circumscribe the range of actions that other government agencies would otherwise have taken in their own interest.

Despite these strategic efforts, the EPB, up until early 1979, was not successful in persuading President Park to reverse direction and slow down the pace of heavy and chemical industrialization. This policy about-face was made only several months before his assassination. In April 1979, having come to grips with the serious consequences of rising inflation, President Park shuffled his cabinet and picked a politician turned health and welfare minister as the new DPM. The latter was given a clear mandate to devise comprehensive policy measures to combat inflation and formulate a new strategy to provide a breakthrough to the economy deep in trouble, both in terms of economic and political stability. What was

---

[23] The development of almost all of the heavy and chemical industries fell within the jurisdiction of the MCI.

[24] There can be a counterargument that the significance of the inflation problem was deliberately exaggerated, since the EPB was not in favor of industrial policy, such as developing heavy and chemical industries from the start. It tried to take advantage of the inflation problem in an effort to occasion a retreat from it. But, as will be seen, this seems to lack historical evidence.

[25] It should be remembered that the EPB housed the Bureau of Statistics, and its analysis was supported by the Korea Development Institute, established as its think tank.

decided on at the Economic Policy Coordination Meeting, presided over by the president himself, was extraordinary. It envisioned scaling-down all major investment plans in an effort to combat inflation, liberalize imports, and accelerate the pace and growth of welfare spending. Unfortunately, however, President Park was assassinated in December that year, before the new plan could be put into effect.

But the plan survived, in spite of President Park's death and the political turmoil that ensued in its wake, and formed the backbone of the incoming government of Chun Doo-hwan.[26] During this political transition, the EPB came to consolidate quite successfully a new economic policy position that it had long favored, that is, a greater market-oriented economic system that would include fairly open foreign trade and the enforcement of fair trade regulations. The question is: How could the EPB make its new economic policy direction survive in the politically tumultuous period and put it in place firmly afterward?

In a period in which major economic policy change took shape, one person who played a pivotal role was the economist Kim Jae-Ik, formerly a director-general level official in the EPB and known as a leading advocate of economic stabilization and liberalization in his ministry and beyond. He was recruited to serve as a key advisor on economic policy affairs for General Chun, and later as his ESP. It is said that he literally inculcated in Chun—who turned out to be a good and faithful student—the philosophy of the free market economy. And President Chun put into practice almost all the elements of the reform package suggested by Kim and the EPB, including the liberalization of import markets and the financial sector. The slogan of Chun's government policy was "economic stability first," replacing the policy of "economic growth first" that marked President Park's era.

It is important to consider the reasons why President Chun depended so heavily on his ESP, Kim Jae-Ik, and the EPB (Lee 1991). President Chun acutely felt the need to distance himself from his predecessor, President Park, and his policy legacies, such as over-investment in heavy and chemical industries, that left a huge nonperforming debt and put a great deal of stress on the banking system. The task of correcting the policy legacies of the previous government could not but be entrusted to those economic ministries that were part of these legacies. Over two decades, ministries such as the MCI and MOF had intervened deeply in the economy. The EPB, naturally, was no exception. But in contrast to these ministries, the indirect nature of the EPB's intervention, its institutional autonomy, and consequent flexibility, permitted it to break free of these legacies more quickly and easily. In a sense, the macropolitical change increased the value of the EPB's distinctive institutional characteristics, namely, its institutional autonomy and consequent policy flexibility.

The second reason that the EPB's economic policy reform survived was the rise of liberal economists in several key economic policymaking positions. When a transition in government takes place, new officials inevitably enter. A more

---

[26] General Chun Doo-hwan, a leading protégé of President Park, took power through an insurgency in the aftermath of the assassination of President Park, and repressed by force the strong resistance against his usurpation of political power.

important question, therefore, is why and how certain like-minded people came to hold the center of the economic policymaking machinery. Two facts stand out: First, Shin Hyun-hwak, the last DPM who served President Park, brought in advocates of economic stabilization and liberalization within the EPB and promoted this group of people within the EPB to hold positions in which they could work as they had wished to. Kim Jae-Ik was a prime example.

The ESP too, at least in this critical period, was so influential that he, instead of the DPM, in effect masterminded the entire decision-making structure and process. The reason behind this was the boundless confidence and trust that President Chun placed in Kim Jae-Ik.[27] The relationship between the DPM and the ESP thus went into reverse, only to return to normalcy in the later years of Chun's government,[28] a development that ought to be welcome. According to Porter, the tendency of presidential secretaries to act as policy advocates should be understood with caution.[29] To the degree that they identified themselves closely with a particular policy alternative, they could not be expected to seek a wider range of policy alternatives or take necessary measures and precautions in dealing with different views and positions. The shortcomings of their taking a particular stand may have been far greater in a political regime like that of Korea in which—with the exception of a small number of technocrats in the executive branch—other legitimate players, such as key members of the ruling party, were not regularly invited to participate in the presidential decision-making process. As the opinion of the presidential secretaries tended to be circumscribed by the president's personal interests, preoccupations, commitment, and beliefs; their other important roles, such as presidential guardian and policy manager, would be inevitably impaired.

The second ESP was a case more in point. As policy matters related to the heavy and chemical industry drive multiplied, President Park decided to use a second ESP by recruiting an official of the MCI at the level of assistant minister who would assist him and work concurrently as head of the working party of the Heavy and Chemical Industrialization Planning Council. The practice of having two ESPs—the first responsible for economic policy matters in general and the second for specific tasks commissioned by the president—was extraordinary, and it has never been repeated since, evidently because of the reasons stated earlier in this section. The moral is that when a president prefers to be involved personally in his pet programs, as was the case with the heavy and chemical industrialization, it is

---

[27] A writer who depicted the structure and process of economic policymaking during Chun's rule called his book "With Respect to the Economy, You Are the President," emphasizing the extent of the confidence President Chun had in Kim Jae-Ik.

[28] It was so especially after Kim Jae-Ik accompanied President Chun on a state visit to Burma and was killed by a bomb that North Korea had set in the national cemetery that President Chun was due to visit.

[29] For a definition of the roles of the presidential secretary, see Porter (1980: 73–83).

likely to put a coordinating agency, such as the EPB, on the defensive and impede its unique and distinctive role as "protector of the national interest."

3.5 The EPB's Demise and the Subsequent Never-Ending Experiments

Although the EPB played a pivotal role in institutionalizing a liberal economic order in the 1980s, its fate was becoming increasingly bleak. Evidently, the loss of its progenitor and protector, President Park, provided this occasion. The EPB was begining to be surrounded by adversaries from all sides. From other ministries and bureaucrats, who had long been ridiculed or overridden by it, the EPB was blamed for frustrating valuable government programs for reasons they could hardly accept. Politicians who had grudges against it, because it had thwarted the budget requests for their constituencies, did not hesitate to bring charges against the EPB's tendency to disregard political accommodation. The presidents following General Park by and large failed to appreciate the value of the role that the DPM could have played for them. President Chun, for instance, tended to communicate directly with the ministers himself, rather than ask them to consult with the DPM and get the latter's preclearance.[30] He somehow seemed to agree on the then prevailing view that the time had gone when the DPM and EPB were required to lead the pack of economic ministries and coordinate economic and industrial policies.

Encouraged by the unfounded charges against the EPB and DPM, President Chun even went so far as to declare that there was no more need for other ministers to consult with the DPM for preclearance because he—President Chun— would personally make the crucial decisions. But this bold initiative was short-lived, as he came to understand before long that the practice of decision-making at the highest levels had grown out of his control and could not work the way he wanted it to. He soon issued a presidential decree that, in effect, reinstituted the preclearance procedure. This tendency was also true of the next president, Roh Tae-woo. Both were former military men and knew almost nothing of economic policy, and had no other feasible alternative than to rely heavily on their ESPs and DPMs in making economic policy decisions. Unlike President Park, they tended to count more on their ESPs than DPMs. Nonetheless, the practice of making and coordinating economic policy by relying on the DPMs for leadership was resuscitated again and again under the rule of the two ex-military presidents.

---

[30] Another reason may be that, on account of his longtime military experience, President Chun may have believed that it would be better for him to communicate with field officers individually and make his decision in front of them in order to leave an abiding impression that he was a decisive leader.

It was not until the advent of genuine "democratic" government that the time of real trial for the EPB began.

President Kim Young-sam of the so-called "civilian government"—a term deliberately chosen to distinguish his government from the previous three authoritarian ones led by ex-military officers—considered the option of dissolving the EPB, which he regarded as one of the institutional legacies of President Park.[31] Faced with conflicting views and opinions for and against the EPB during the transition period, he postponed the decision, while putting part of his government restructuring plan into effect. On returning from an Asia–Pacific Economic Cooperation summit in Indonesia in November 1994, President Kim—nearly 2 years after his inauguration—suddenly made public his plan to further reorganize the government, the notable part of which was the dissolution of the EPB and the status of the DPM entirely. The alleged purpose was to change the mode of economic policy management to make it more adaptive to trends in globalization. The EPB and the MOF were merged into a new Board of Finance and Economy (BOFE), a mammoth ministry and the largest in the history of Korea.[32] Worse still, President Kim designated an ex-finance minister as the first minister of BOFE, reflecting his complete lack of knowledge about the institutional uniqueness of the EPB and the service it had uniquely provided for the presidents and the nation.

In brief, the merger of the EPB and the MOF into the BOFE meant a significant loss of institutional autonomy that the EPB had enjoyed. Within the BOFE, the MOF's operating responsibilities began to take precedence over—or overshadow, or at least impair—the coordinating functions played so well by the EPB. Most of all, the virtual loss of the center of economic policymaking and coordination was not simply a problem left unresolved for long, but one which eventually exacted a high price. Although it was supposed that the minister of BOFE would play that role, he lacked formal authority. Worse yet, other ministries that came to have a taste for independence were reluctant to cooperate with him. To the extent that the ministers of other operating ministries could persuade the president, there was no need for them to consult with the head of BOFE. By then, the national assembly tended to cut into the budgetary process. Even though it was only a natural political development, the BOFE was not well prepared to deal with this political intervention competently. In addition, as Korea became a member of the Organization for Economic Co-operation and Development in 1996, its economic policy in general, and foreign exchange policy in particular, had begun to be circumscribed. In these circumstances, the Korean economy fell victim to the contagion of an

---

[31] President Roh Tae-woo was also elected democratically under the new constitution, which had been entirely revised in the aftermath of the massive civic movement for democratization in 1987. The claim of President Kim Young-sam that his government ought to be the first "civilian" government was unjustified, except for the fact that Roh was a man from the military.

[32] Through the reorganization in December 1994, the Fair Trade Commission and the Bureau of Review and Evaluation, which had been housed in the EPB, were moved to the Office of the Prime Minister.

economic crisis that had started in the Southeast Asian region in 1997, which necessitated the intervention of the International Monetary Fund.

While it is not easy to substantiate, the author contends that Korea may have been able to obviate the crisis if the EPB had remained in place and played its customary role. In the latter half of 1997, a rumor went around that Korea might be the next victim. But no preventive action was taken. If the EPB had been present, it would have seriously heeded this warning signal from the international financial community and taken necessary steps, including realigning the foreign exchange rate, even in the face of political resistance, because it had the public credibility to do so. Unfortunately, however, it was the very action that the BOFE was highly reluctant to take for political reasons, which seemed also to be the case with President Kim Young-sam. The year 1997 was, after all, a presidential election year, and the Korean people—buttressed by an overvalued *won*—indulged in overspending abroad. Whatever the real causes of the economic policy debacle and the accountability for it, it marked the beginning of government restructuring aimed at improving the workings of the economic policymaking and coordination apparatus in Korea.

Tracing briefly what happened thereafter, the BOFE, as the ministry most accountable for the unprecedented economic policy failure, became a leading target in the government restructuring undertaken by incoming president Kim Dae-jung in February 1998. The BOFE was reduced to the Ministry of Finance and Economy (MOFE), while its budgetary authority and functions as a whole were moved to the newly established Agency for Budgeting (AFB), which continued to be under the jurisdiction of MOFE. The AFB was designed to work in line with, and under the general supervision of, the Presidential Commission on Planning and Budget (PCPB). Subsequently, in 1999, in the name of improving the efficiency of budgetary functions, the PCPB and AFB were joined to become the Planning and Budget Agency (PBA). But this was not the end of the story. The next president, Roh Moo-hyun, again reorganized the government and strengthened the PBA by incorporating new functions which were largely the remainder of those held by the EPB, but had ended with its demise. In an effort to facilitate the integration and coordination of related policy areas, President Roh revived the title of DPM and conferred it this time not only on the minister of MOFE, but also on two others, the ministers of unification and education, respectively. But the attempt fell far short of expectations. By this time, the fame and power of the DPM was past. Again, the next president, Lee Myung-bak, reshuffled the government entirely from the start, and established the present Ministry of Planning and Finance, while abolishing the status of the DPMs altogether.

What did this inconvenient series of reorganizations aimed at reviving different sorts of coordinating functions in lieu of the EPB mean? First, it provided convincing evidence that there exists a constant need for an effective economic policy coordination mechanism, even though it is hard to find an alternative to the one centered on the EPB. The decision of President Kim Young-sam to force the EPB offstage was mistaken, since it was based on a misunderstanding of the sources of the EPB's institutional strength. Mindful as he was of getting rid of any legacies of authoritarian rule, President Kim and his advisors failed to understand the institutional uniqueness of the EPB. This had almost nothing to do with political and bureaucratic authoritarianism. Instead, the EPB's accomplishment was commendable, even in fully democratic countries, in the sense that it was achieved in the workings of policy competition among government agencies. The EPB's achievement resulted not from anything authoritarian but from its proven excellence in the wrangle of policy competition. The EPB tended to win out over other ministries almost always by logic rather than fiat. The frequently voiced opinion that the EPB had been predominant only reinforces the author's argument: If a coordinating agency falls short, it simply means that it fails to perform its coordinating role well.

Second, as mentioned earlier in this section, the reason for forcing the EPB offstage was to change the mode of economic policymaking and coordination so that it would be more appropriate in adapting to the globalization trend. But it should have been understood that it was the EPB that proved most sensitive and responsive to new changes, demands, and developments of any kind and deserved some attention in charting the future course of development. For instance, it was the EPB that first turned the nature of planning from directional to indicative in response to the growth of the private sector. It was also the EPB that—among other achievements—brought social welfare policy into the framework of economic development planning, and strengthened the structure and process of international economic policy coordination in the face of rising trade friction. This can only mean that the EPB was sacrificed for no solid reason other than that of political symbolism.

3.6 Conclusion

It may be only natural that incoming presidents wish to restructure the government. The reasons for doing so are varied. Szanton groups them into six categories. These include (a) shaking up an organization to demonstrate decisiveness, or simply placing his or her mark on it; (b) simplifying or streamlining an organization; (c) reducing costs by minimizing overlap and duplication; (d) symbolizing priorities by giving them a clear organizational embodiment; (e) improving program effectiveness by bringing separate but logically related programs under a unified direction; and (f) improving policy integration by placing competitive or conflicting interests within a single organization or subjecting them to processes of coordination.[33] Whatever the reasons for reorganization may be, so Szanton argues, the reorganization effort scarcely lives up to expectations. Instead, the costs incurred may well outweigh the benefits. But there seems to be a tendency to

---

[33] Szanton (1981: 2–3).

prefer major structural change to other approaches, such as changes in decision-making processes. The former, though, is apt to be costly, painful, and difficult to accomplish, while the latter is inclined to be easier to achieve and more useful. Changes in processes that seek to ensure better and more effective coordination are the most broadly appropriate as well as the most feasible forms of organizational change.[34]

Viewed from this perspective, Korea can be singled out as a prime example of attempts at government reorganization occurring most frequently, even in cases where changes in the decision-making process would have been more appropriate than major structural changes. For over 60 years since independence, Korea has witnessed over 50 attempts at government reorganization, and it is difficult to tell which of them has been successful and which not. But there is at least one exception, that is, the establishment of the EPB, in which structural change and changes in the decision-making process had been combined in a most satisfactory way.

Effective coordination is hard to achieve because it is difficult to get agencies to do things against their own interests, and there are organizational impediments to effective management. It is no surprise, therefore, to see so many cases of coordination failure that were weak and unstable, time-consuming, and exhausting. This was not the case with the EPB, however. The EPB was neither feeble nor weak. Its decisions were made swiftly and decisively, and its implementation was particularly effective. In this respect, the EPB was a rare success case. It was created by the military coup leader, General Park, in 1961 as part of his government reorganization. To the extent that reorganization affects the distribution of power among government agencies greatly,[35] it certainly helped the EPB to stand out vis-à-vis other economic ministries. It is a gross misunderstanding to consider the EPB's power and influence as if they had sprung from reorganization per se. Emphatically, this was not so. It was an acquired, rather than simply vested, asset and quality.

The EPB's success as a government agency responsible for drawing up economic development plans and implementing them effectively was an outcome of good governance concerned with coordination, a happy amalgam of authority and responsibility. The EPB profited to a substantial degree from the status of the DPM, a special title conferred on its minister, and budgetary resources placed largely at its disposal. But at the same time, and more importantly, the EPB was charged with immense and unprecedented responsibility to coordinate all economic and industrial policies in support of the economic development plans, and the EPB carried out this responsibility dutifully and effectively. What made the EPB play its role with such effectiveness and competence?

The author contends that the key to this question is to be found in the confidence that the presidents placed in the DPMs and the EPB, and the degree to which the EPB was successful varied with the strength of their confidence. For

---

[34] Szanton (1981: 8).

[35] For a discussion of the political meaning of organizing as a powerful source affecting the distribution of power, see Seidman (1981: 33–57).

example, during the 18 years of President Park's rule, the DPM and EPB predominated in the major economic decision-making process. By contrast, during the next 15 years—comprising the administrations of Presidents Chun and Roh, and the early half of the administration of President Kim Young-sam—it was the ESP that played a more powerful role than the DPM, while the talent and expertise of the EPB was, as before, fully harnessed by the ESPs.[36] This contrast seemed to stem from the fact that President Park personally wanted to be involved as deeply and fully as he could in the process of economic development, to which he was strongly committed, while the two succeding presidents had neither the passion nor the economic knowledge to lead as competently as President Park had done.

The single most important reason for President Park's confidence in the DPM and the EPB was the broader scope of mission that the DPM and EPB had learned to come up with, and it proved to be of great service to the president who thought of himself as chief executive officer on whose shoulders the fate of the nation rested.[37] Their broad scope of mission in turn led the DPM and EPB to have a more comprehensive and longer term perspective on economic and industrial policies. And this, in turn, necessitated their building up extraordinary organizational assets, including strategic managerial skills, and expertise, in addition to pride and self-confidence. Although no explicit thought was given to the makeup of the EPB, except equipping it with budgetary functions to make the incipient planning system work more efficiently,[38] the EPB happened to find itself being institutionally autonomous. This institutional autonomy proved to be a fundamental and critically important factor in making the policy positions and solutions that the EPB proffered look more independent and objective. It also served as the fountainhead of policy flexibility, which turned out to be even more important in the sense that it enabled the EPB to conduct its mission in the face of constantly changing internal and external economic and political conditions. With this self-reinforcing mechanism at work, the EPB's power and influence grew quickly, and persisted.

It was, therefore, unfortunate that the EPB was sacrificed at the altar of political democratization. As argued in Sect. 4.5 the decision to force it offstage in 1994 was completely erroneous. This is well supported by the fact that the never-ending experiments in government reorganization in search of the role and functions that the EPB had played so well, but now in different organizational forms, have all turned out to be unsuccessful. The EPB's power and influence diminished in the

---

[36] It should be remembered that all the ESPs were chosen from the high echelons of the EPB, with rare exceptions from the MOF.

[37] Hwang (2011: 283–313).

[38] There seems to be no such vestige of thought that to make the EPB powerful and influential it should be given institutional autonomy. The available evidence suggests that to lend effectiveness to the planning system, it must be accompanied by budgetary power. This argument has been criticized by the present author because this could not have been a sufficient condition for the EPB to play its role effectively and competently, given the general truth that budgetary functions tend to be easily subject to political interference.

process of political democratization as tolerance for authority generally decreased and the power of special interests and the single-issue politics grew. Certainly it is not an organizational matter, but a matter of politics. However, structured, staffed, or budgeted, institutions cannot wield a power that political forces deny them. But institutions may be well or poorly designed to exercise whatever potential they have.[39]

In this sense, one can argue—as the author has done—that the institutional characteristics of the EPB are of the sort that may have to be appreciated more properly than ever before.

The author does not suggest that the developing countries need to model their economic policymaking structure and process after Korea's. But this chapter contains some policy and organizational concerns that ought to be addressed whenever these countries try and forge a working relationship among key economic policymakers and an economic policy coordination mechanism that works effectively and competently. The most prominent concern perhaps is that the governance structure must be set up in such a way that a ministry like the EPB can enjoy institutional autonomy and hold center stage. The author suspects that its importance will probably grow with political development in developing countries.

References

Barzelay, M. (1986). *The politicized market economy: Alcohol in Brazil's energy strategy.* Berkeley, CA: University of California Press.

Choi, B.-S. (1987). *Institutionalizing a liberal economic order in Korea: The strategic management of economic change.* PhD dissertation, Harvard University, June.

Cole, D. C., & Nam, Y. W. (1969). The pattern and significance of economic planning in Korea. In I. Adelman (Ed.), *Practical approaches to development planning: Korea's second five-year plan.* Baltimore, MD: Johns Hopkins Press.

Hirschman, A. O. (1958). *The strategy of economic development.* New Haven, CT: Yale University Press.

Hirschman, A. O. (1979). The turn to authoritarianism in Latin America and the search for its economic determinants. In D. Collier (Ed.), *The new authoritarianism in Latin America.* Princeton, NJ: Princeton University Press.

Hwang, B. (2011). *The Park Chung Hee paradigm.* Seoul: Chokwang Press.

Jones, L., & Sakong, I. I. (1980). *Government, business, and entrepreneurship in economic development: The Korean Case.* Cambridge, MA: Harvard University Press.

Kim, H. K. (Ed.). (1999). *The glory and shame of the Korean economy: A secret history of 33 years of the economic planning board.* Seoul: Maeil Kyungjae Shinmun.

Kim, Y. H. et al. (Eds.). (1987). *Anatomy of Korean economic policies in the 1960s and 1970s: The interaction of government and business in economic development.* Honolulu: East-West Population Institute.

Lee, J.-K. (1991). *With respect to the economy, you are the President.* Seoul: Joongang Ilbo.

Lindblom, C. E. (1965). *The intelligence of democracy: Decision making through mutual adjustment.* New York: The Free Press.

---

[39] Szanton (1981: 7).

Mason, E. S. et al. (1980). *The economic and social modernization of the Republic of Korea*. Cambridge, MA: Harvard University Press.

Porter, R. B. (1980). *Presidential decision making: The economic policy board*. Cambridge: Cambridge University Press.

Schick, A. (1981). The coordination option. In P. Szanton (Ed.), *Federal Reorganization*, op. cit.

Seidman, H. (1981). A typology of Government. In P. Szanton (Ed.), *Federal Reorganization*, op. cit.

Szanton, P. (Ed.). (1981). *Federal reorganization: What have we learned?*. Chatham, NJ: Chatham House Publishers, Inc.

Chapter 4
Bureaucratic Power and Government Competitiveness

Tobin Im

4.1 Introduction

How did the bureaucracy in Korea manage to empower the nation's talent and mobilize its scarce resources so efficiently toward economic development, especially in the 1960s? Korea's spectacular economic growth has attracted the attention of practitioners from many developing countries, but few in-depth studies have been carried out focusing on the special role that the bureaucracy played in this process. While there are many factors that contribute to a nation's development and one factor alone cannot in isolation explain completely the phenomenal success of Korean industrialization, the country's bureaucrats have nevertheless played an important role greatly deserving of independent examination.

This chapter starts from the premise of a bureaucratic development model. It builds on the argument that a developing country can successfully leverage a strong bureaucracy as a tool to cope with the lack of other national endowments—such as institutional maturity, wide leadership pools, or the prevalence of natural resources—that may otherwise aid in the process of economic growth. More specifically, this chapter describes how the formation of the Korean bureaucracy and the direction of its organizational evolution have allowed it to play an authoritative and even dominating role vis-à-vis other state and non-state actors. The key questions to be explored are how the bureaucracy acquired its substantial power and how it used this power to transform an anarchic and unstable state into a highly productive engine of economic growth.

Government bureaucracy is a typical example of an organization formed for the deployment of resources to achieve strategic goals, and as such, is a key variable

T. Im (✉)
Graduate School of Public Administration, Seoul National University, Seoul 151-742, Republic of Korea
e-mail: tobin@snu.ac.kr

H. Kwon and M. G. Koo (eds.), *The Korean Government and Public Policies in a Development Nexus, Volume 1*, The Political Economy of the Asia Pacific, DOI: 10.1007/978-3-319-01098-4_4, © Springer International Publishing Switzerland 2014

in determining outcomes that even start from the same set of resources. This chapter will focus on the organizational aspects of the Korean government that led to high levels of efficiency and effectiveness.

4.2 Formation of the Bureaucracy in a Korean Context

Korea has a long tradition of placing ethical and competent officials in positions of government power, putting the country in the mandarin tradition during the Chosun Dynasty, which lasted over 600 years from the fourteenth to the twentieth centuries (Cha and Im 2011). With Confucian principles guiding administrative and societal ethics, human relations were defined hierarchically so as to simplify interpersonal relations in society. Age, social status, or belonging to a certain group were, consequently, the decisive factors in deciding interpersonal conflicts. These hierarchical principles are still embedded in the mentality of ordinary Koreans. As such, Hofstede (1981) argues that current Korean society is characterized by high power distance (60 points), collectivist social behavior (18 points for individualism), and femininity (39 points for masculinity)—features also emphasized by Kim in her 2006 study. While these proposed features should not be accepted without scrutiny, what should be stressed from an organizational perspective is that the relationship between public officials and citizens is hierarchical, with the state able to discipline and greatly influence the behavior of non-state actors (Amsden 1989), with the guiding metaphor of a paternalistic state governing its children.

Under the Japanese colonial government, the Confucian bureaucratic tradition and its meritocratic system of advancing the most competent individuals to positions of power was extinguished. The Japanese colonial government exploited bureaucrats, especially policemen, in order to extract resources from Korea, particularly for military purposes during World War II (Kohli 1994). The Japanese government divided Koreans into a relatively small number of collaborators by giving ruler's job such as police for example and non-collaborators and oppressed inhumanly the majority population. This resulted in a very negative perception of public administration. Due to a distortion in the incentive system, the civil service during this difficult period was plagued by high levels of corruption, and public officials—or collaborators—no longer worked in the public interest. As a result, not only did the long tradition of a civic-minded and competent state vanish, a general trust in state bureaucrats disappeared with it.

After a successful coup d'etat in 1961, Park Chung-hee, a major-general in the Korean armed forces, emerged as leader of the government and quickly initiated a modernization program throughout the bureaucracy (Haggard et al. 1993), a process which is still underway today. Park advertised his intention to clean up the bureaucracy by eliminating sources of corruption, but also recognized that much of the talented bureaucrats were not entirely free from the taint of collaboration with the Japanese. He attempted and largely succeeded in reforming the bureaucracy, making it more centralized and authoritarian, with himself at its center, and in many ways sought to imitate what he had seen as the efficient functioning of the military formed under the influence of the United States (US) army. Building on these values, Park was able to quickly create a vastly more efficient and focused bureaucratic organization than had existed before his accession to power.

Scholars have tended to give Park a lion's share of the credit for the modernizing that took place during this period, and indeed it cannot be denied that he personally was behind many of the modernization programs. Nevertheless, one individual cannot be responsible for a change of this particular magnitude. Scholars of public administration also exerted a significant influence on the direction of institutional development and the shape of government organizations. For example, the role of the Graduate School of Public Administration—founded in 1959—at Seoul National University was to produce scholars intent on importing into Korea administrative theories drawn largely from the American context. Seeking to broaden its influence in the southern half of the peninsula, the US State Department sponsored master's or doctoral studies for dozens of law graduates of Seoul National University. These US-trained scholars actively engaged in government reform programs as external consultants, or on diverse presidential commissions, or by educating future high-ranking officials (Graduate School of Public Administration of Seoul National University 2009, p. 14). Especially influential was professor Cho Suk-choon, whose primary focus was on organization theory. US-trained professors like Cho and others came to stress the principles of administrative management in the tradition of Gulick and Urwick (1937).

The formation of Korean bureaucracy is a mixture of these conflicting cultures. On one hand, the traditional hierarchical relations in Korean society played a central role in shaping human relations throughout the government, while on the other an intellectual climate dominated by reformers—newly steeped in the classics and contemporary literature of American public administration scholarship—continually pushed for greater reforms. Elucidating this conflict and tracing its impact on the future of Korea's central government organization is the main purpose of this chapter.

Government bureaucracy can be understood as an organizational mechanism aimed at coordinating a diversity of societal actors with the intention of producing positive change in society. In many developing countries, government is the most "powerful" or "organized" organization within society, and much depends on the ability of individuals working for the government to effectively deliver on select goals that the nation must achieve in order to advance to a higher level of development. Government service in Korea has always been treated as a highly honored profession, and an elevated social status is conferred upon individuals who rise through its ranks. This level of prestige was reflected in the relative privileges extended to government employees during President Park's administration, including benefits such as full medical insurance and a generous national pension at a time when such benefits were unthinkable for the average citizen (Kwon 2002). But relative privilege aside, the manner in which civil servants were organized in order to carry out their tasks is another question for organizational specialists to answer.

Government organization needs systematic control and coordination mechanisms by which to ensure that the various ministries and government organs do not work at cross-purposes or pursue goals different from those set by the central administrative body (Chibber 2002). Whether to create a ministry to deal with a new mission was a primary question during the rapid developing period, but a more important issue was to whom this coordinating power was to be given fro the organizational point of view. The major government work to be done following the Korean War (1950–1953) largely involved rebuilding the fundamental infrastructure of the country and was funded primarily by foreign aid, chiefly from the US (Minns 2001). This process was not a particularly efficient or effective one, however, and the lack of a clear set of development goals beyond basic stabilization, as well as the absence of a uniform bureaucratic organization, prevented any significant advancement of the common good.

This want of coherence and operational efficiency in the government bureaucracy was a key concern of the newly established Park Chung-hee regime. Consequently, in 1962, an Economic Planning Board (EPB) was established and given immense power within the bureaucracy to coordinate the actions of the ministries. Because of its central position organizationally, as well as the fact that the president himself closely communicated with its head, the EPB effectively monopolized economic policymaking power within the government bureaucracy in the early days of the authoritarian regime. Besides the president himself, other members of the EPB were mostly graduates of Seoul National University who were highly motivated to make a substantial shift in the country's trajectory by leading its development strategy (Yu 1976). Under the direct guidance of Park and the EPB, government organizations and institutional arrangements in the country were formed with the singular goal of economic development. This swift transformation from a loose structure with poorly defined goals into a highly centralized, highly focused bureaucracy with a militant level of discipline is the hallmark of Park's impact on the development of government organization in Korea.

4.3 The Golden Principles of Managing Organizations

Once the size of an organization grows beyond a certain ceiling, managers need to think of its organizational structure from the viewpoint of efficiency, as organizations of significant size present different challenges than do simpler and streamlined groups. Classic organization theories, and those of the administrative management school in particular, have focused on discovering universal laws for managing large organizations. Typical examples are Follett (1924), Gulick (1937), Weber (1947), Fayol (1949), Urwick and Brech (1949), and Barnard (1968). Principles such as the separation of lines of staff, chain of command, unity of command, span of control, centralization versus decentralization, and criteria of departmentalization are among the important elements of organizational science.

This section will discuss some of the fundamental principles as understood from the classical perspective. These principles were born in the time of the scientific management movement when industrialization was accelerating and Western economies were experiencing higher productivity than ever before. A philosophy of maximum efficiency underlay each of the principles, and reform movements that aimed at elaborating these golden standards within the organizational context continue today. In general, it can be said that Western organizational theories value operational rationality and focus on efficiency in public management. More detailed knowledge of this category is being reproduced and spread to developing countries in various ways, and governments have now begun to adopt such management techniques as benchmarking, specialized training, and academic exchanges.

This chapter aims to challenge the dominant Western tradition of academic research with regard to its applicability to the Korean case. Korean bureaucracy has always been very hierarchical and even authoritarian, which is a counterexample to the theoretical model mentioned in the previous paragraph. It has also been very centralized and characterized by narrower spans of control than would seem necessary, in accordance with Western-originated theories. Nevertheless, the organizational structure and culture in Korea have produced remarkable results in a relatively short time, lending weight to the argument that Korean-style organization—though not based on the golden principles of management—has nevertheless produced a highly effective and efficient structure. Moreover, because of this underlying alternative culture, there is a significant gap between what Western-inspired textbooks say and what the bureaucrats think.

There is no "one best way" to organize government bodies, regardless of a country's economic situation or internal resources. Several central questions are posed here, a fundamental one being whether Gulick's theory of administrative management can apply to the Korean government. Administrative management scholars continue to offer recommendations for managers on how to organize a company, or government, to make it more efficient. The question can be refined as follows: in the case of Korea, have the recommendations of the unity of command, ideal span of control, departmentalization, and decentralization been necessary for the efficiency of the government bureaucracy and the development of the country?

4.3.1 Chain of Command

The chain of command principle relates to the unbroken line of authority that links all persons in an organization. Specifically, it regulates who reports to whom in an organization. This principle is associated with two underlying ones, namely, those of unity of command and scalar chain. Unity of command means that one subordinate cannot receive orders from more than one senior if smooth operational efficiency is to be maintained. This rule recommends a single line for the chain of command which links the top manager to the street-level bureaucrat. The scalar principle means that all organizational members should be included somewhere within the hierarchical ladder without exception. The morphology of a big organization must, therefore, take a pyramidal form if the chain of command is to be strictly applied in organizational design.

The chain of command principle concerns the formal and legitimate power of a manager to make decisions and issue orders. This authority is distinguished from other forms of power in the sense that it is accepted as legitimate by subordinates who will execute it, according to Weber's definition (Weber 1947), and it is vested in organizational rank rather than in individuals. The chain of command rule should be complemented by the principle of delegation. Delegation transfers a degree of authority and responsibility from superiors to subordinates while maintaining the superior's position as an individual ultimately responsible for the actions—and their consequences—of subordinates. Working on the assumption that those closer to a given problem will have a better understanding of it, and will then make the most appropriate decisions on how to deal with it, modern organization theories recommend that managers delegate authority to the lowest level possible, and as often as possible (Lee and Choi 2006, p. 86; Daft 2010, p. 308).

4.3.2 Line and Staff Authority

Since the time of Adam Smith, it has been understood that an organization's efficiency can be increased through the specialization of individual tasks. This specialization enables employees to focus on a narrower area of work in a repetitive way, thereby developing a higher degree of competence at their work. While jobs tend be small, the organization becomes more efficient. In terms of the relations among these employees, at least two kinds of authority are operational. Line authority is given to individuals in management positions who have the power to direct and control immediate subordinates, while staff authority is granted to staff specialists in their areas of expertise. For example, directors, bureau chiefs, and section chiefs are line authorities who make decisions and sign successively along a hierarchical ladder. But the director adjoint and chief adjoint or auxiliary chiefs in bureaus are staff authorities who do not make decisions but help their respective superiors by working in the capacity of secretary. In addition to augmenting efficiency, this specialization of tasks and the corresponding forms of managerial control aim to facilitate communication in large organizations.

4.3.3 Span of Control

Span of control refers to the number of subordinates who report to a supervisor. Organizational theories have long attempted to find an ideal span of control. Although there is no uniform number on which there is agreement, it has been suggested that—optimally—seven is most suitable. Recent studies, however, show that this can vary, depending on the nature of the task, employee or supervisor capacity, environmental uncertainty, and other factors (Van Fleet and Bedeian

1977). With the advent of information technology in organizations, the number of subordinates a manager can effectively supervise has again increased.

The span of control that is used in an organization determines whether the organization is tall or flat. There is an inverse relationship between span of control and the number of hierarchical levels in a given organization. For example, in order to supervise 4,096 employees at the operative level, a managerial hierarchy could be organized more economically. With a span of four, an organizational level of seven would require 1,365 managers at levels 1–6 to manage the 4,096 employees. But with a span of eight, an organizational level of five would require only 585 managers at levels 1–4 to manage the same number of employees (Robbins 2001). This means that a taller structure would need to hire 780 middle managers more than a flat one (i.e., 1,365–585 = 780). The tall structure has a narrower span and more hierarchical levels, while the flat structure has a wide span and is horizontally dispersed with fewer hierarchical levels. In other words, the tall structure needs to pay for a larger number of managers and often limits subordinate discretion. In addition, there can be problems of communication between the top and street-level echelons. For instance, if it is assumed that about 10 % of information is lost each time it passes through a hierarchical ladder, the top manager in the hierarchy will have significantly less information; the manager at level eight will receive 0.53 % of the total information that started at the lowest level; while a manager at level five will receive 0.66 % of it. This is the reason why recent researchers tend to recommend flatter organizations.

4.3.4 Centralization and Decentralization

Decentralization devolves power to subordinates by making them quasi-autonomous entities. This relates to how much power the top manager or the central government monopolizes in comparison with other employees or organizational bodies. In particular, the more widely dispersed an office is geographically, the greater the need to decentralize. But many problems that arise from great geographical distances can be overcome with the help of advanced transportation and communication technologies.

The necessity for decentralization comes from the uncertain environment in which an organization is located. The more rapidly changing and uncertain an environment is, the more difficulty a centralized organization faces (Daft 2010). In government organization, there are two kinds of decentralization: political and administrative. Political decentralization is about giving policymaking power to local governments by introducing local elections, for example, while administrative decentralization—or deconcentration—aims to give some discretion to local governments in the implementation stages of policies designed by the central government.

Modern Occidental theories of management tend to recommend reforms in favor of decentralization as much as possible (Im 2010). There is a contradictory relationship between centralization and decentralization. All conditions being equal, centralization facilitates efficiency in strictly implementing policies created at the center, while decentralization facilitates flexibility in implementing policies in response to local realities. If it is a relation between the top manager and subordinates in an organization, decentralization seems similar to delegation. The difference between decentralization and delegation is that the former extends power almost completely to subordinates, while the latter preserves the leadership's power over activities delegated.

4.4 The Case of Korea's Government Organization

The formation of the Korean bureaucracy and its organizational development would not have been possible without the ideological support of Western-oriented theories of public administration. Alongside the economic development process, public administration as a university discipline thus came to play an important role in enlarging and changing the way of thinking of members of the bureaucracy. Scholars fluent in the English language worked tirelessly to disseminate Western theories and as such became supporters, as well as teachers, of government bureaucrats. This symbiotic relationship between academia and practitioners is remarkable for its consequences, as the first generation of faculty of the Graduate School of Public Administration were able to see the ideas that they proposed from reading American and Western literature being directly applied to the bureaucracy, with visible results (Chung 2007).

For example, the government—on the basis of recommendations by Korean scholars—formalized its management structure using a Western-style organization chart. This method of determining a set of formal tasks which define the division of labor in a ministry, as well as the framework of vertical control and formal reporting relationships, allowed bureaucrats to understand their organizational reality in a methodical way. In the process, they could isolate inconsistencies that might produce problems for the smooth execution of bureaucratic power. The production of an official organizational chart was a major step in developing the formal underpinnings that led eventually to a highly efficient organizational structure of the government during the country's development.

Mirroring the single focus of government action in the early days of development, the organization of government in the 1960s was simple, with the number of ministries in 1963 being 13 (Fig. 4.1).

The functions of government have expanded remarkably ever since. Even though the Lee Myung-bak administration had declared its intention to streamline government organization by consolidating existing ministries, the organizational chart (Fig. 4.2) continues to show a high degree of complexity. But this growth of functionality and structure should not be attributed to bureaucratic expansionism and the ambition of entrenched bureaucratic interests (Niskanen 1971, pp. 22–30). Over the past 50 years, the gross national product has grown 280 times

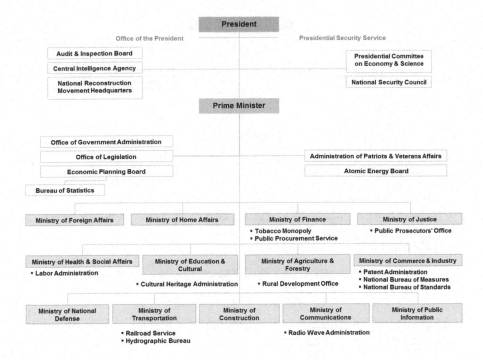

Fig. 4.1 Government organization chart 1963

and the volume of exports has risen 10,000 times. It is natural that growth of this magnitude be accompanied by some expansion in both the size and scope of government, as the resources needed to effectively govern in a modern and complex economy are themselves complex. Relative to many other states of similar economic size, the Korean government organization is substantially smaller and more streamlined, which means that the government has been relatively successful in stopping the tendency toward rapid organizational growth. The size of the Korean government is roughly one-third of the average for countries of the Organisation for Economic Co-operation and Development, although this comparison is problematic, considering the differences in public sector and definitions of civil servants among these countries (Kim 2000).

It is within this organizational context that the application of the golden principles of organizational management can be examined, and their effectiveness evaluated (Table 4.1).

4.4.1 Application of the Principle of Chain of Command

When General Park took power in 1961, Korea ranked as one of the poorest countries in the world, without a well-organized government bureaucracy. As a two-star

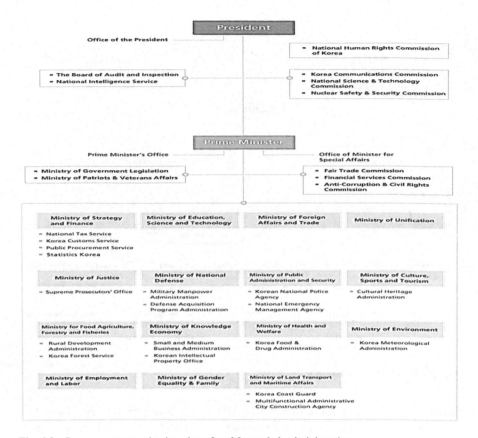

Fig. 4.2 Government organization chart, Lee Myung-bak administration

general in the Korean military whose operation was influenced largely by the US army which was stationed in Korea since the liberation of the country from Japan, and which played a critical role in the Korean War, President Park led the government bureaucracy with a functioning military organization in mind. The Korean military, especially after having experienced the war, was the best example of a chain of command in practice. The ruling mentality was that nothing was impossible and that subordinates could execute any order given to them by any means necessary.

That the chain of command be upheld as strictly as possible was a foremost concern of President Park on attaining office. The president was like the commander in chief of the Korean government organization; ministers were generals; directors were colonels; and so on down the line. The goal of the war was the country's economic growth, and enlarging exports was set as the strategy. The main scheme for achieving this goal was the Five-Year Economic Development Plans which were implemented in the annual budget in a more detailed way.

President Park himself regularly checked the implementation status of these plans and visited industrial areas frequently. Monthly meetings on export

Table 4.1 Korean economic performances

Planning stage	Unit	1st		2nd		3rd		4th	
		Plan	Outcome	Plan	Outcome	Plan	Outcome	Plan	Outcome
Rate of economic growth	Annual average (%)	7.1	7.8	7.0	9.6	8.6	9.2	9.2	5.8
Unemployment rate	"	8.5	7.6	6.1	5.0	4.2	4.1	4.0	4.1
GNP deflator ascension rate	"	–	19.7	–	14.9	–	21.4	8.8	20.0
Consumer price ascension rate	"	–	19.7	–	15.0	–	15.9	–	18.6
Total amount of currency increase rate	"	–	30.6	–	47.2	–	31.1	24.5	24.7
Export increase rate	"	28.0	38.6	17.1	33.8	22.7	32.7	16.0	11.1
Import increase rate	"	8.7	18.7	6.5	25.8	13.7	12.6	12.0	10.5
Total amount of balance of current account	Billion dollar	0	–0.3	–1.4	–2.7	–3.1	–4.9	–1.9	–15.2

Source Kang (2000)

promotion were occasions where the president was informed of the performance of various sectors, and solutions to any obstacles to the achievement of these goals were discussed. The president strongly reproached whoever was responsible for the obstacles, and it was a widely shared feeling that those answerable did not want to disappoint the president. To find whoever was responsible, the principle of the unity of command was highly useful because it showed clearly who received the order from whom, and who did not implement the order.

This clear structure of accountability, central to the early regime's organizational ethos, could not last indefinitely. As the size of the Korean economy expanded, so too did the size of the bureaucracy that was instrumental in guiding it, and the president himself became too busy to check all the details of this performance game, as had been his preference earlier. The number of immediate collaborators grew, and while central power continued to be a defining organizational feature, more authority was needed to be delegated throughout the organization. In order to maintain the centrality of organizational power and the chain of command that supported it, Park came to rely more and more on a small group of representatives who would act as his *avatar* in meetings and planning sessions (Kim 2011). Thus, even with increasing organizational complexity and a multiplication of fundamental tasks that the bureaucracy pursued, the unity of command remained a central feature of bureaucratic organization.

4.4.2 Korean Version of the Principle of Separation Between Line and Staff

The reporting system of top and street-level bureaucrats was almost perfect, to the extent that there was a clear line of command from the president down to the ministers, governors, mayors, and bureau chiefs of local branch offices, as well as to bureaucrats at the street-level. The president could call at any time in order to question an appropriate individual and obtain the information necessary because of this clear and tight unity of command. This was especially effective in implementing policies that the president considered a priority. The president also tended to appoint former generals to line positions as heads of key ministries, such as justice, the interior, construction, and so forth.

This government structure was filled by various staff units. The presidential office was the typical staff unit for the president. The Blue House staff was for President Park a sort of quasi-cabinet, with the equivalent of a minister at its head who presided over senior-level secretaries, each responsible for overseeing one or two ministries under them to turn the central government's development vision into reality (Kim 2011). Kim (2011) points out that because Park relied on other government organs—particularly the Korean Central Intelligence Agency—to handle political matters, the Blue House staff was remarkably apolitical in its outlook, and was therefore able to focus its entire energy on implementing central directives.

In addition to the more traditional presidential office, the EPB (see Sect. 4.2 above) was created in 1961 and strengthened in 1962, and became a powerful staff organization within the government structure. This staff organ was conceived of as a think tank that established, for example, strategic planning measures, including the important five-year plans, and played the role of overall policy coordinator (Cheng et al. 1998). The elite group working for this small and centralized agency, always able to access the president, was rivaled only by the Ministry of Finance (MOF), the previous center of government (Im 2010, p. 261). However, the EPB had certain privileges that made its board the more powerful of the two. First, the EPB had the final say over the national budget, and hence had an advantageous negotiating position vis-à-vis the MOF in shaping ministerial priorities (Cheng et al.1998). But more importantly, because foreign finance was the primary source of income in the early developmental years, and the EPB had the authority to seek and secure foreign loans, it was largely independent of the influence of the MOF, and could set national development goals without having to seek domestic funds through the finance ministry.

President Park worked more closely with the EPB by giving it the power to implement decisions. Within the government bureaucracy, the EPB took advantage of its power to allocate budgets and played a lead role in accelerating all ministerial activity toward the nation's economic growth. Formally or informally, it was the EPB, acting with effective oversight of the president, that issued the orders to government organizations in this regard. The head of the EPB was to be elevated to the rank of deputy prime minister, which illustrates his influence in the government. Curiously, the prime minister's role was more symbolic than real, so that, in this sense, the head of the EPB could be considered the second most powerful man, next to the president.

This practice of a staff body, rather than an individual, issuing orders to line employees goes against the golden rule of clear separation between line and staff. The same phenomenon was to be found inside each ministry where subunits, such as sections and bureaus, were organized in accordance with the line-staff principle. In other words, the principle was applied to the formal organization, but staff units were inclined to intervene in the hierarchical line in the informal process of operation. This can be termed "linization of staff," which results in the informal addition of hierarchical sections to an organization. One positive example is the head of the EPB mentioned in the previous paragraph. But a linization of this type appears to be a negative side effect which can arise in an extremely efficient organization.

Effective implementation within an agency needs an able staff organization, as the problems that an organization deals with become complex and difficult to solve. As this requires highly qualified personnel, human resources development becomes the reverse side of the coin. The president himself turned out to be an enthusiastic learner in regard to the country's development. Having a bureaucracy organized along military lines was insufficient to realize his dream of developing the country. It seems, therefore, that he actively sought out the few Koreans who had obtained advanced degrees in universities in the US and offered them good research environments in an attempt to lure them back to Korea, as many successful scholars had already emigrated from the country. It is in this context that the Korea Institute of Science and Technology was founded through the president's personal attention. Acutely aware of the lack of skilled human resources, the president emphasized the education and training of civil servants. Confucian culture also encouraged young Koreans to do their best to study. As a result of this insistence on training and high education, an elite group in the bureaucracy—comprised mostly of graduates from Seoul National University—made their appearance.

4.4.3 Application of Span of Control

The classic recommendation of a span of control of seven has not been applied in the case of the Korean government. Korea's bureaucracy has always been a tall structure, to the extent that there are nine grades in the civil service system. Civil servants, mostly career seekers, tend to add higher positions as many as possible in order to increase the chances of being promoted. This great eagerness for rapid promotion has uniformly reduced the official span of control to three, which is narrow (General Regulation of Government Organization and Total Number of Government Employees, Presidential Decree 14438).

A tall structure with a uniform span of three at all levels of a hierarchy requires more managers than a flat one. This means that everyone prefers giving orders and managing to implementing orders at the street level. The more managers there are in an organization, the less efficient the organization becomes. There are few competent operatives, while the most capable employees are in a managerial position. More managers than subordinates does not make for a healthy and efficient organization. In order to create high positions, there is a tendency to ramify public bodies whose function focuses more on a specific area. Creating a public, or parapublic, organization conveys the effect of generating more positions, since it requires a head and an administrative unit, which would be unnecessary if it were not set up. This tendency toward bureaucratization is the flip side of Korean bureaucracy, which has been excellent in implementing orders throughout the development era.

The positive effect of this bureaucratization is to stimulate civil servants by offering them a relatively rapid promotion path up the hierarchical ladder. In other words, self-actualization—the highest human need, according to Maslow's theory of needs—is more easily satisfied in a tall rather than flat organization with fewer promotion opportunities. Some civil servants have climbed from the bottom to the top, or ministerial, position within 20–30 years of service. Their exaltation comes from this extraordinary career process, which the author calls the "roller coaster effect" (Yu and Im 2012, p. 341). These extremely motivated officers had done their best to develop new strategies of development for the country's economy and made sure of their implementation. Being a high civil servant was considered the epitome of social success for the younger generation, and the civil service entrance examinations continue to give equal opportunity to every youth, regardless of social background.

However, the proliferation of high positions, as well as the ramification of similar organizations, led to in the problem of coordination at the top level, especially the presidential level. Agencies in the government competing with each other would defer to the president to decide difficult policy issues that they could not agree on at their own level. For example, the relationship among ministers became more and more conflictual as they tried to monopolize important issues in order to exhibit their competence to the president. In other words, the span of control for the president had passed the limit within which the running of an efficient and responsive bureaucracy was possible. Despite the growth of the presidential office—the Blue House and its staff—this trend appeared unavoidable.

Thus, the principle of span of control turned into one of span of attention resulting from bottlenecks in the flow of information. Having the president's personal attention was considered a sign of being recognized as an important entity among rival agencies. The first rank collaborators—ministers, for example—used every possible opportunity to secure the president's support for their policy ideas. *Naerak* and *NaeInga* are typical cases in point, spawned in this context of the power game(Cho and Im 2010).

4.4.4 Naerak (Informal Consent)

The informal consent system of the Korean government refers to the custom of asking for the Blue House's consent in regard to the content of any policy. Most commonly, the term is used to request the president's approval for the appointment of senior government officials.

4.4.5 NaeInga (Preliminary Authorization)

The system of preliminary authorization is similar to that of informal consent in that it also involves requesting the president's consent on official matters. It refers to the custom that highly values the president's preliminary authorization, despite the legal power of authorization regarding any public relations or legal agreements residing in each administrative body. For example, items that have not received this preliminary authorization are not included in the agenda during cabinet meetings.

None of these two systems is legally binding, but is more a custom that has been followed for decades, and continues even today. The two arose as derived form from the span of attention which is a kind of the span of control principle when applied to a busiest leader such as the president. These customs are perhaps deeply connected to the old Korean adage, "one crawls on one's own." The saying refers to people who, after considering their level of power, will decide to avoid any conflict with those who have more power than them. This decision is self-made, based on calculations of any future profit or loss that may stem from the relationship with the other actor. Hence, those in a superior position do not necessarily need to exercise their power as their inferiors will not challenge them in the first place.

4.4.6 Centralization Versus Decentralization

It is undeniable that bureaucracy in Korea has been extremely centralized around the president as well as the Blue House, as the *Naerak* and *NaeInga* traditions explained above show (Sects. 4.4.4 and 4.4.5). President Park and his two successors were especially notorious for their dictatorial style, and despised for it by their democratically-minded opponents outside of the bureaucracy. The unity of command in the administrative line was neatly established from the president to the street-level bureaucrat, as mentioned earlier (Sect. 4.4.2). Until 1994, governors responsible for upper-level local authorities and mayors were just employees of the interior ministry. Local elections were not established until the decentralization reform in the 1990s.

It is worth noting that local branch offices of ministries of the central government have proliferated, with their mission being mainly to assure implementation of the central government's policies. These organizations are hierarchically aligned to the extent that subordinate organizations faithfully and unilaterally execute a superior organization's directives and guides. In particular, villages in rural areas have their chiefs, and there are leaders of dozens of households in urban areas as well. These grassroots leaders form an important link between formal administrative organizations and ordinary citizens (Im 2004, p. 74). In the middle of each month, representatives of these households (i.e., the lowest administrative circumscription) gather together to share information on government policies. Some criticize these meetings as a dimension of government propaganda because they began at eight in the evening by watching a government program aired by the Korean Broadcasting System. But the meetings also serve to enhance public information diffusion among citizens. The grassroots organizations work together with the *saemaeul*—"new community"—movement in a complementary manner. In this way, the central government's administrative actions have penetrated the lives of ordinary citizens. The incredible effectiveness in the field that has characterized the performance of Korea's bureaucracy has been possible because of this high degree of centralization and its incorporative elements.

4.5 Good Governance in Developing Countries

Democracy does not have one universal and strict meaning, but has evolved numerous versions which can be found throughout the world. Democracy as a political institution originated in Europe and has developed over centuries. The key debate has been around the concept of sovereignty, and shifting sovereignty from the ruler to the people took place neither quickly nor without much resistance.

The essence of modern democracy is best summarized in Abraham Lincoln's famous phrase of government for the people, of the people, and by the people. In modern times, this became a fundamental philosophy and unquestionable value. However, applying these principles at the same time to non-Western countries can be problematic. Specifically, the third—or government-by-the-people— principle is more or less important, depending on a nation's historical and political situation. In fact, democratic institutions in the West are designed to fulfill this principle. One of these is indirect democracy, which relies on people's representatives, and the other is direct democracy, which emphasizes people's participation in policy-making processes instead of relying on their representatives. Today's trend is to lay more stress on direct, rather than indirect, democracy.

4.5.1   Limits of the Principle of Government by the People

Indirect democracy was believed to be a technically feasible means of bringing about democratic values when direct democracy did not work, for whatever reason. But indirect democracy is also criticized due to the principal-agency problem for example, especially if the problem relates to information asymmetry (Arrow 1963). As communications technology develops, and people's consciousness grows, representative democracy increasingly becomes a target of criticism. Incompetence, political corruption, and bureaucratic dysfunction especially aggravate the criticism of representative democracy and lead individuals to search for alternatives. For instance, referendums on important issues are a tool for mitigating the weaknesses of indirect democracy. Scholars go further in emphasizing citizen participation, to the extent that they advocate replacing the concept of government by governance (Peters and Pierre 1998).

Nevertheless, there are two questions that must be answered by proponents of more direct frameworks of democracy. First, is the crowd capable of making good policy, and if so, under what conditions? And secondly, is it possible for a multitude of citizens to participate in policy decision-making processes without any distortion of their will? Any such mechanism to aggregate their wills may result in Arrow's paradox (Im 2008, p. 157) and true public sentiment will not be expressed. While "deliberative democracy" seems well-suited to incorporate the values of citizens in an inclusive way by allowing the diversity of citizen preferences to adjust to an equilibrium (Cohen 1997), it is not yet clear how such a communicative framework is to be designed wherein this process could take place.

But a more fundamental question regarding the applicability of Western democracy can be posed as far as developing countries are concerned. Many developing countries do not, as they begin the reform process, have any form of efficient government, that is, a competent bureaucracy capable of realizing the government-by-the-people principle. Several experts on developing countries, who advocate the introduction of the concept of governance, report frustration with the incompetence of existing government bodies (Jakubiak 2004). But governance is defined as co-decisions between government and civil society in making and implementing public policy (Chung 2005), which emphasizes the end of the state's monopolistic position. The question to raise here is whether a governance system can be operated in a developing country where there is no well-institutionalized government and mature civil society. In this case, which may be considered the norm in developing countries, governance without government makes little sense.

A developing country needs at least a locomotive institution to initiate and implement relevant policies. Government organization is the legitimate institution that best fits this locomotive role. However, governments in many developing countries are fragmented, corrupt, incompetent, and do not dispose of resources in an efficient manner. Even if civil servants are notorious for these negative qualities, it is realistic to see that the real power of a government needs to be invested in a coherent bureaucracy. Bureaucracy as an organization of civil servants must be the key actor in developing countries. Governance can be introduced only from the time that government works and manifests its monopoly of power. Therefore, the first question is how a correctly working bureaucracy can be institutionalized.

Korea's experience clearly demonstrates that government bureaucracy is considered to have played a locomotive role in the economic progress of the country. In a sense, Korean bureaucrats formed one of the most competitive groups in the world in the sphere of guided economic growth. The organizational phenomenon seen in Korean bureaucracy is peculiar in many senses, but ultimately under-researched.

Civil servants were privileged with a relatively high salary and medical insurance, as well as a pension plan, which were unthinkable for ordinary citizens of the period. They were an elite who understood the strengths and weaknesses of the Korean economy, considering its natural and human resources. They themselves were also rare resources who had studied in foreign countries and thereby gained the knowledge on which they could build development strategies for Korea. They were accurate and punctual in implementing these strategies to meet their development goals.

4.6 Conclusion

Developing countries in almost every case lack an efficient organizational apparatus that can effectively use human resources and motivate national growth. Even resource-abundant countries that lack this essential tool appear to be unable to leverage these assets and raise the general conditions of society—a weak and failing state being held hostage to special interests and incapable of asserting its will through policy. As Korea does not possess any natural resources of note, it can be said that the rapid pace of development took place only through the ingenuity and tenacity of its citizens. Even so, it is doubtful whether Korea's transformation from one of the world's poorest nations to a world leader in many significant categories could have taken place without a strong state encouraging its citizens to act in their country's longer term interest.

Several conditions made it possible for President Park and his military collaborators to take and hold power with the endurance that characterizes developmental administration. First, the Korean War engendered chaos in society, and the existing hierarchical social order was shaken to such an extent that many established interests vanished as significant sources of entitlement. Everyone was equal, in a sense, to race for success.[1] Second, at an international level, the US found in Park an ally in its campaign to contain communism in the region, and hence, despite the authoritarian nature of the state during his tenure, political and economic support was available from a hugely powerful ally. These factors gave the Park administration an exceptionally high degree of autonomy vis-à-vis society (Johnson 1987), which seemed to hold out few opportunities for the country's talented youth outside of a career in the civil service.

Another condition that cannot be overlooked is the organizational leadership of Park himself. While the list of authoritarian leaders in the modern history of the state is by no means short, Park threw himself into his role with boundless energy and an unswerving commitment to national development that became a major source of organizational power (Cho and Im 2010). Nevertheless, Park was never quite the dictator that his enemies made him out to be. He wielded the power that he did because of the efficient and focused bureaucratic apparatus that this power flowed through. In the end, it is difficult to distinguish the power of an individual from the organizational mechanisms through which it is exercised.

This culture of hierarchy and organizational submission, however, is also not in and of itself a sufficient condition for an agency to be successful in attaining its goal, in this case development. Chibber (2002) argues that organizational adherence to bureaucratic principles and rules may even produce the opposite effect if individual agencies do not have any single body coordinating their policy from a neutral standpoint. In this situation, scarce resources, and the goals of individual organs, may create undue competition and even conflict within the government organization, ultimately leading to an inability to act as a unified machine. It is this situation that the Park administration was able to avoid through the combination of careful organizational design and adherence to hierarchy.

In developing countries, a diverse selection of social and political forces can hinder state capacity and consequently cause it to act in disunity. In these situations, the capacity of the state must first be reinforced and even isolated from the various partisan interests of the greater population. One way to increase the capacity of the state is to mold it into a strong bureaucracy, as was done to great effect in the case of Korea. However, while the introduction of the golden principles of

---

[1] Land reforms throughout the Syngman Rhee presidency—just prior to President Park's—not only offered up much of the rural population for industrial labor, but also destroyed what was left of a hereditary landholding class, thus eliminating another source of potential adversaries for Park and his administration (Kwon and Yi 2009).

organizational management will all create organizational value in the right context, reformers must take care that this context is indeed the one that they are working in. Secondly, the contemporary emphasis on governance is destined to fail if introduced into a country which does not already have a fully functioning organizational structure capable of operating on its own. This chapter does not take issue with any of the golden rules, nor the idea that value can be created through the greater participation of citizens in the policymaking and implementation process. Rather, it challenges the universality of these rules as well as the non-temporal dimension that those who support them would inscribe them with.

A major source of bureaucratic power for Park and the developmental administration was the particular configuration of ministries and government organs at the highest to the lowest levels. In particular, ministries were segmented according to their policy importance and Park would not let ministries of the first order, like the EPB, the MOF, and the Ministry of Commerce and Industry be used for anything other than their missions, preserving positions in the lower and less instrumental ministries for cronies and conspirators (Cheng et al. 1998). Thus, as crucial as hierarchy was to the individual relationships within the bureaucracy itself, ministries themselves were organized hierarchically, with those at lower levels incapable of doing much damage if they were to step out of line.

References

Amsden, A. (1989). *Asia's next Giant: South Korea and late industrialization*. New York: Oxford University Press.

Arrow, K. J. (1963). *Social choice and individual values* (2nd ed.). New York: Wiley and Sons.

Barnard, C. I. (1968). *The functions of the executive*. Cambridge, MA: Harvard University Press.

Cha, S., & Im, T. (2011). Network analysis of the Uijeongbu decision making system in the Chosun Dynasty. *Korean Journal of Policy Studies, 20*(4), 447–478.

Cheng, T.-J., et al. (1998). Institutions and growth in Korea and Taiwan: the Bureaucracy. *Journal of Development Studies, 34*(6), 87–111.

Chibber, V. (2002). Bureaucratic rationality and the developmental state. *American Journal of Sociology, 107*(4), 951–989.

Cho, S.-c., & Im, T. (2010). *Theories of Korean Government Organization [in Korean]*. Seoul: Bupmunsa.

Chung, Y. (2005). The Pursuit of Korean governance paradigm: governance and national capability. The Korean Association for Public Administration Winter Conference, 2005.

Chung, Y. (2007). The life and thoughts of Professor Park Dongseo: in terms of public administration of Korea. The Korean Association for Public Administration Summer Conference, 2007.

Cohen, J. (1997). Procedure and substance in deliberative democracy. In J. Bohman & W. Rehg (Eds.), *Deliberative democracy: essays on reason and politics*. Cambridge, MA: The Massachusetts Institute of Technology Press.

Daft, R. L. (2010). *New era of management*. Mason, OH: South-Western Cengage Learning.

Fayol, H. (1949). *General and industrial management*. London: Pitman.

Follett, M. P. (1924). *Creative experience*. New York: Longmans, Green and Co.

Graduate School of Public Administration of Seoul National University. (2009). *Fifty-year history of the graduate school of public administration of Seoul National University*. Seoul: Seoul National University.

Gulick, L. H. (1937) Notes on the theory of organization. In L. H. Gulick & L. F. Urwick (Eds.), *Papers on the science of administration* (pp. 81–89). New York: Institute of Public Administration, Columbia University.

Haggard, S., Cooper, R. N., & Moon, C.-i. (1993). Policy reform in Korea. In R. H. Bates & A. O. Krueger (Eds.), *Political and economic interactions in economic policy reform: Evidence from eight countries* (pp. 294–332). Cambridge, MA: Blackwell.

Hofstede, G. H. (1981). *Cultures and organizations: Software of the mind*. New York: McGraw-Hill.

Im, T. (2004). *Organizational research on the local Government of Korea*. Seoul: Bakyoungsa.

Im, T. (2008). *Global public ethics*. Seoul: Bobmoonsa.

Im, T. (Ed.). (2010). *Decentralization and development: the Korean experience*. Seoul: Seoul National University Press.

Jakubiak, K. (2004). Tell Farama (Pelusium): preliminary report on second season of Polish-Egyptian excavations. *Polish Archaeology in the Mediterranean, 16*, 60–68.

Johnson, C. (1987). Political institutions and economic performance: the government-business relationship in Japan, South Korea, and Taiwan. In F. C. Deyo (Ed.), *The political economy of the new Asian industrialism* (pp. 136–164). Ithaca, NY: Cornell University Press.

Kang, K.-H. (2000). *The five-year economic development plan: Evaluation of policy goals and enforcement*. Seoul: Seoul National University Press.

Kim, B.-K. (2011). The Labyrinth of solitude: Park and the exercise of Presidential power. In B.-K. Kim & E. F. Vogel (Eds.), *The Park Chung Hee Era: the transformation of South Korea* (pp. 140–167). Cambridge, MA: Harvard University Press.

Kim, S. (2006). Public service motivation and organizational citizenship behavior in Korea. *International Journal of Manpower, 27*(8), 722–740.

Kim, T. (2000). Comparing Bureaucracy size in Korea and OECD Countries. *Korean Journal of Public Administration, 34*(1), 117–135.

Kohli, A. (1994). Where do high growth political economies come from? The Japanese lineage of Korea's "Developmental State." *World Development, 22*(9), 1269–1293.

Kwon, H.-j. (2002). Welfare reform and future challenges in the Republic of Korea: beyond the developmental welfare state? *International Social Security Review, 55*(4), 23–38.

Kwon, H.-j., & Yi, I. (2009). Economic development and poverty reduction in Korea: governing multifunctional institutions. *Development and Change, 40*(4), 769–792.

Lee, C., & Choi, C. (2006). *New organizational theories*. Seoul: Daeyoungmunwhasa.

Minns, J. (2001). Of miracles and models: the rise and decline of the developmental state in South Korea. *Third World Quarterly, 22*(6), 1025–1043.

Niskanen, W. A. (1971). *Bureaucracy and representative Government*. Chicago, IL: Aldine-Atherton, Inc.

Peters, B. G., & Pierre, J. (1998). Governance without Government? Rethinking public administration. *Journal of Public Administration Research and Theory, 8*(2), 223–243.

Robbins, S. P. (2001). *Organizational behavior*. Upper Saddle River, NJ: Prentice Hall.

Urwick, L. F., & Brech, E. F. L. (1949). *The making of scientific management*. London: Management Publications Trust.

Van Fleet, D. D., & Bedeian A. G. (1977). A history of the span of management. *Academy of Management Review, 2*(3), 356–372.

Weber, M. (1947). *The theory of social and economic organization* (A. M. Henderson & T. Parsons, Trans.). New York: Oxford University Press.

Yu, H. (1976). Tasks of graduate school of public administration for public administration. *Korean Journal of Public Administration, 14*(2), 2027–2039.

Yu, M., & Im, T. (2012). *Public personnel management: In terms of Government competitiveness (in Korean)*. Seoul: Bakyoungsa.

Part II
Public Policies for Development

Chapter 5
Governing the Developmental Welfare State: From Regulation to Provision

Huck-ju Kwon

5.1 Introduction

The transformation of the Republic of Korea (hereinafter referred to as "Korea") over the past 50 years has been impressive, if not miraculous, even to unconcerned observers. Once one of the world's poorest countries Korea's fast economic growth has turned it into a society that is both modern and affluent. Its ruthless authoritarian regime has yielded to elected governments in a stable but vibrant democratic polity. Equally important, but less noticed in Korea's remarkable metamorphosis, has been the evolution of the welfare state. The welfare state in Korea progressed from a simple structure with a minimal number of programs to a fairly comprehensive system (Ringen et al. 2011). During this time, the country acquired distinctive social policy characteristics which changed it into what the author calls a "developmental welfare state" (Kwon 2005). This refers to an institutional arrangement of the welfare state where elite policymakers set economic growth as a fundamental goal, pursue a coherent strategy to achieve it, and use social policy as an instrument to attain that goal. In other words, the developmental welfare state comprises a group of social policies and institutions that are predominantly structured to facilitate economic development.

In this regime, social policy is regarded as an instrument for economic development, giving priority of social protection to those with strategic importance for industrialization, while leaving the poor and vulnerable outside the welfare system. How, then, did Korea manage to keep social inequality in check, and at a relatively low level, during its rapid economic development? It is a combination that other emerging economies, such as China and Brazil—recent Asian and Latin American success stories—have not been able to replicate. What were the social dynamics and public institutions that enabled Korea to reduce poverty and

H. Kwon (✉)
Graduate School of Public Administration, Seoul National University, Seoul 151-742, Republic of Korea
e-mail: hkwon4@snu.ac.kr

H. Kwon and M. G. Koo (eds.), *The Korean Government and Public Policies in a Development Nexus, Volume 1,* The Political Economy of the Asia Pacific, DOI: 10.1007/978-3-319-01098-4_5, © Springer International Publishing Switzerland 2014

maintain social equality? In this chapter, the author pays particular attention to the governance of the welfare state in Korea in the early years of social policy development, from the 1960s to 2000s. This chapter will track the evolution of the governance of the welfare state to accommodate changes to it, from its establishment and expansion to its consolidation.

There have been two important landmarks in the development of Korea's welfare state: the initial introduction of a few social welfare programs in the early 1960s and the Asian economic crisis of 1997–1998. In the early 1960s, the government of Park Chung-hee, which took power in a military coup in 1961, set up the basic structure of governance through the 1970s. As will be discussed in this chapter, the Park government used social policy as an instrument for economic development. The other significant factor that influenced the characteristics of the welfare state in this period was the democratization that took place largely in the 1980s.

The second period of the growth of the welfare state began with the Asian economic crisis. During this crisis, the weakness of the developmental welfare state in Korea was painfully exposed, as its economy was among the hardest hit. The unemployment rate soared to a historic level of 8.6 % in 1999, from 2.6 % in the previous year. This was due mainly to a high incidence of business failures during the economic crisis, and also to the structural reform of the Korean economy to make it high-technology oriented and globally competitive. These economic imperatives led Korea to choose to strengthen its welfare state at a time of economic crisis, which went against the conventional, neoliberal wisdom of the day. The welfare state became more inclusive with the integration of the fragmented National Health Insurance (NHI), the introduction of a Minimum Living Standard Guarantee (MLSG) for the poor in 2000, and the extension of an employment insurance scheme in 1999. These were parts of the Kim Dae-jung administration's efforts to establish a welfare state based on social rights.

How did industrialization and democratization affect the governance of the welfare state? And what kinds of changes were brought about in the administrative structure of the welfare state in order to accommodate this transformation? In attempting to answer these questions, this chapter will first discuss the analytical framework to examine the governance of the welfare state, and then consider the social and political structure of Korean society from the 1950s to the 1970s, which set the macro-context of social policy. Next, it will seek to provide a detailed analysis of governance structures at each stage by examining social policy interventions in the two main periods of social policy development.

5.2 Two Modes of Welfare State Governance: Regulator and Provider

In the economic development of Korea over the past five decades, the state has played a strategic role, which can be grasped by the conception of a developmental state (Woo 1991). In doing so, the Korean state settled for economic development as its foremost priority, which led to a social policy system that could be instrumental in its development. For instance, social insurance for large-scale industrial workplaces was first introduced to protect workers. In this sense, the welfare state in Korea can be described as a developmental welfare state (Kwon 2005). In establishing this, the state played a crucial role, but not the same as in other countries, as one might expect. For instance, the role of the state in Korea was different from the role of the state in many European countries. This chapter will elaborate on the modes of governance for social welfare. The state may provide social protection in the form of services or finance, or regulate social actors to render social protection.

In his previous work, the author attempted to enlarge on two different modes of governance in a welfare state (Kwon 1997). The first mode is the state as provider. As in the typical national health services in Sweden and the United Kingdom, the state provides social services and benefits, which are paid for through state expenditure. In other words, the state is a direct provider of social welfare. The second mode of governance is the state as regulator. In this mode, the state imposes regulations under which other social actors provide social welfare. For example, employers are forced by regulation to participate in public insurance for their workers, who have also to contribute to the program. The private service providers are regulated to make social protection and services available to citizens. In this mode of governance, the state neither finance social welfare programs with its own resources, nor does it use its institutions to provide services. It only regulates others.

There are many differences in governance between the two modes (see Table 5.1). First, in terms of finance, social welfare is supported by taxation in the provider mode, while social insurance contributions are the main source of funding in the regulatory mode. Second, public institutions deliver social services in the former mode, while private institutions supply welfare services in the latter. Third, in the provider mode of governance all citizens are basically entitled to services, while in the regulatory mode only those who have paid contributions for a certain period of time are entitled to services. Fourth, in the provider mode, the state has to have the ability to finance and run social programs directly. Nevertheless, it is still necessary for the state to set up institutional frameworks that can implement regulations, although—in the regulatory mode—there are fewer institutional requirements. Lastly, redistributive outcomes are larger in the provider mode than in the regulatory one. What is the underlying reason for adopting one mode of governance over another? In contrast to the provider mode of governance, the state—in its regulatory mode—can implement social

Table 5.1 Modes of welfare governance

Role of the state	Provider	Regulator
Finance	Taxation	Social insurance contributions
Social welfare delivery	Public institutions	Private institutions
Entitlement	All citizens	Contributors only
Administration	Governmental agency	Quasi-governmental agency
Redistributive effects	High	Low

policy programs in an incremental manner and be selective in terms of coverage. However, the state should be able to "regulate" other social actors as well.

The remainder of this chapter will examine the governance of the welfare state in Korea and trace changes that have occurred in its transition from the first to the second period. The chapter will argue that the mode of social policy governance in Korea has been closer to the regulatory mode in the first period. Thereafter, the state had begun to assume, to an increasing degree, the role of provider during the expansion of the welfare state in the wake of the Asian economic crisis. This contention inevitably raises an important question: if civil servants and workers employed in strategic industries were among the first to be protected by social policy programs in order to mobilize them for economic development (Yi 2007), how was Korea able to combine economic development and poverty reduction? Economic growth does not necessarily lead to poverty reduction, while social policies tend to have little impact on poverty reduction and income inequality. Once Korea strengthened its welfare state in order to include those who had been outside the system, how could it maintain economic competitiveness despite the rising social cost of welfare? It is necessary to answer this question about the social structure before moving to the governance of the developmental welfare state.

5.3 Multifunctional Institutions and Social Welfare Before Industrialization

Prior to discussing the introduction of social policy in the 1960s, when industrialization took off in Korea,[1] one needs to look at the structural basis of the society in which Korea embarked on economic and social development that led eventually to economic growth and poverty reduction. The country's state-led economic development was labor-intensive, and poor but well-educated workers responded to the government's efforts at industrialization. In the process of economic development, the Korean state had a considerable degree of autonomy with regard to vested interests, such as the landowning class. The relative autonomy that the state was able to exercise stemmed from its land reform after independence in 1945, which was carried out from the late 1940s to the early 1950s. Land reform also provided a political economy in which a poverty-stricken society such as Korea was able to have well-educated and disciplined workers before industrialization took off.

After the liberation from Japanese occupation in 1945, the sovereign Korean government (established in 1948) promulgated laws on land reform in 1949, in response to socialist land reforms in North Korea. It was a political effort to counter socialist movements and undermine the economic basis of the dominant

---

[1] This section draws largely on Kwon and Yi (2009). "Economic Development and Poverty Reduction in Korea: Governing Multifunctional Institutions." *Development and Change* 40, 769–792.

landowning class (Sin 1988). Given the fact that the Korean government had just been established—following the end of Japanese occupation—it was not an easy task for the newly independent government to carry through on land reform. These reforms led to an increase in the number of small farmers who owned their land for farming and the reduction of inequality in landownership. The second effect was a dramatic rise in mass education in the 1950s–1960s. Families in rural areas, who now saw higher productivity on their own land than when they worked on it as farm labourers, could now send their children to school instead of the paddy field. The Korean government also placed a high priority on education, next only to defense. This meant that young people in rural areas were well-educated long before the industrialization project was embarked on (Cho and Oh 2003). In brief, these young workers participated in a mainstream change of society—that is, through industrialization—and the results of economic growth could be shared widely among the Korean population.

If land reform was effective social policy in the 1950s, the Korean government mobilized other public institutions to reduce poverty in the 1960s. For instance, the widespread practice of usury in rural areas was banned in 1961 by the Park government. In times of poor harvest, farmers often borrowed money from moneylenders at high interest rates. This usurious practice often pushed farmers into chronic poverty due to the high rates of interest. Such practices were banned, and existing loans had to be registered at local agricultural cooperatives. These cooperatives, which issued bonds to moneylenders with lower interest rates, took the place of moneylenders in rural areas. In effect, the ban and regulation were a partial cancellation of loans to poor farmers. Together with land reform, government regulation gave farmers the opportunity to work for themselves and be independent.

Other institutional features that worked effectively as social policy were the local health centers. The government created these centers, which spread out across the country, to provide basic health services and act as a first defense against infectious disease. Due to fiscal constraints, the government was able to equip the health centers with only the minimal medical facilities, but the centers were operated mostly by young trainee doctors who were granted exemption from mandatory military service. With this compensation structure, the government was able to position the trainee doctors in all public health centers, which in turn were able to provide basic healthcare services to low-income families at little cost.

Another key public move to reduce poverty was the *Saemaul Undong* (or New Village Movement) in the 1970s, a kind of self-help voluntary community initiative. It was a nationwide effort to mobilize human resources for economic development in rural areas, and was organized partly by the government and partly through the voluntary participation of rural communities. After swift industrialization in the 1960s, economic conditions in rural areas fell behind, and the gap in income between urban and rural sectors increased. Against this background, some rural communities organized voluntary campaigns to improve the economic infrastructure of their communities so that they could enhance agricultural productivity. Following initial success, the government stepped into making *Saemaul Undong* a nationwide community drive, providing start-up grants to rural communities to organize their own *Saemaul Undongs*. On average, the government allocated 2.5 % of gross national product each year. People in villages offered their labor voluntarily to the self-help movement, since better infrastructure would be to their advantage as well. In the late 1970s, *Saemaul Undongs* spread to urban areas too. While there was a component of political mobilization for the authoritarian government, it is fair to say that the *Saemaul Undong* was essentially a voluntary movement, which is why it was so successful. It also turned out to be very effective as social policy.

5.4 Regulating Social Policy in the 1960s and Onwards

The modern institutions of social policy were introduced in Korea in the 1960s, mainly by the military government led by General Park. Although the Civil Service Pension Act was introduced in 1960, it was the military government that started to implement it in 1962, with more generous conditions for pensions than previously planned. It was followed by the Military Personnel Pension Act of 1963. This legislation was designed to give protection and security to public personnel who were seen as crucial for the political stability of the government.

5.4.1 Industrial Accident Insurance

But it was the Industrial Accident Insurance in 1963 that clearly indicated the direction of government social policy. As the military government was about to embark on the first Five-Year Economic Development Plan, it saw Industrial Accident Insurance as an essential policy instrument for its 5-year plans. Soon after the 1961 military coup, the government considered various options for social policy, including programs for unemployment insurance, public health insurance, and industrial accident insurance. In the end, it decided to introduce only the Industrial Accident Insurance, first to large-scale industrial workplaces with more than 500 workers, and then—incrementally—to smaller-scale workplaces. The top decision makers believed that Industrial Accident Insurance would provide income support and healthcare to injured workers, while the program's financial responsibility would be placed with firms which, in accordance with labor laws, were legally responsible for paying compensation for industrial accidents.

From a mode of governance perspective, it was very similar to that of the regulatory mode. Industrial Accident Insurance was financed by contributions from employers. Healthcare services for injured workers were provided by private hospitals and clinics. The government only needed to provide administrative support to run the insurance program. This support was given from the start of the program by an insurance department created for the purpose within the Labor Administrative Agency.

5.4.2 National Health Insurance

NHI (known initially as Medical Insurance) shows the most typical characteristics of regulatory governance. It is worth examining the evolution of NHI closely, since it illustrates the nature of the welfare state in Korea. In the early period of the Park government, a public health insurance program had also been considered, together with Industrial Accident Insurance discussed above (Sect. 5.4.1), but was only implemented as a pilot scheme in a few large workplaces. NHI became compulsory in 1977, starting with large-scale companies of more than 500 employees. Firms with fewer than 500 employees could also join, but it was not obligatory for them to do so. Although the initial idea of implementing a mandatory NHI came from the conditionality attached to the United States loan, the government—this time—was prepared for such a program (Park 1979). In 1978, government employees and private schoolteachers became compulsory members, and the number of people covered reached 20.49 % of the population (see Table 5.2). Thereafter, the NHI rapidly expanded its coverage. In contrast, those who had no recognized employers—such as farmers, the self-employed, informal sector workers, and the unemployed—remained outside the scheme. This was partly because of the contribution arrangements under which employers and employees each paid half of the contribution to NHI. (The average contribution rate in 1980 was 1.9 % of wages and—in 1999—2.62 %.[2]) The groups of people referred to above did not have employers who would have paid their portion of the contribution, and the government was not prepared to spend an equivalent share for those without formal employers. There were other reasons for this too, as Mills (Mills 1985, p. 80) explains: "Social Insurance schemes are concentrated in the industrial sector in developing countries not least because wages and profits are high enough for compulsory levies to be paid, and the structure of wage employment makes collection of the levies feasible." This selective approach seems practical when introducing a social welfare program in a developing country that does not have enough public expenditure to pay for such a program, or a well-organized bureaucratic structure to administer it.

The role of the state in NHI in this period typically fits the regulatory mode. The state effected social policy in the form of an obligatory rule under which certain workplaces would have health insurance without financial support. Subsequently, quasi-governmental and health insurance agencies, as insurers, were set up to deal with insurance administration and manage their own health funds. These agencies covered only a small number of workplaces that belonged to similar businesses. There was no one unified national insurance entity at the time, but there were a number of health insurance agencies for industrial workers and an agency for public employees and private schoolteachers. A regulatory—rather than provider—type of financing was more compatible with the selective approach that

---

[2] Wages here refer not to actual take-home pay, but to 35 bands of the standard monthly wage. As of 2012, the contribution rate is 5.8 %.

Table 5.2 Coverage of national health insurance, 1977–1989 (percentage of total population)

	Industrial	Public	Occupational	Regional	Others	Total
1977	10.33	–	–	–	–	10.33
1978	10.34	10.15	–	–	–	20.49
1981	18.70	10.27	0.06	0.47	0.19	29.69
1984	28.75	10.11	2.02	0.97	0.53	42.38
1987	36.01	10.50	3.17	0.76	0.69	51.13
1988	38.76	9.67	2.58	16.15	0.64	67.80
1989	38.96	10.55	0.00	44.69	0.00	94.20

Note Percentage of members and their families respectively
Source National Health Insurance Agency (1990)

Korea had taken. If the state had financed health insurance through public expenditure, it would have been very difficult to justify the selective approach in which only a relatively insignificant number of citizens was included, while others were left out. A simple provider type of financing would, of course, have cost the country a great deal of money, which was not available at the time.

Within a health insurance fund, members paid their contributions at a certain rate of their wages, and there was a redistribution effect between the rich and the poor. This redistribution, however, only took place within—and not across—funds, since each fund maintained its separate financial account. In terms of reimbursement to hospitals, health insurance companies paid hospitals on a fee-for-service basis (Abel-Smith 1994). Most hospitals operating under NHI were private, although not for profit. The Ministry of Health and Social Affairs decided the price of treatments for health insurance agencies each year, after consulting with doctors, hospitals, and economic ministries. There was also a wide range of treatments that NHI did not cover, and the period for which one could use NHI was limited to a maximum of 6 months in any given year. In addition to these measures of cost containment, patients also paid 20 % (as inpatients) to 30 % (as outpatients) of the fee as copayment when they visited clinics and hospitals.

The selective approach to establishing NHI had its fair share of problems. In this period, the membership of NHI became a symbol of the middle class. As the coverage of NHI increased, those outside the program became more isolated from the rest of the population. They also shared a common characteristic in that they were not salaried employees. While some of them might be well off, most belonged to low-income groups. When nonmembers visited a hospital, they found two queues, one for NHI patients and the other for non-NHI patients. They also had to pay more for their treatment than NHI patients, who paid only 30 % of the fees.

Health Insurance funds were instituted in the 1980s for groups of the self-employed and, consequently, NHI expanded rapidly. In 1981, when the National Health Insurance Law was amended, occupational associations of the self-employed could organize health funds within NHI. The National Association of Artists put together a health fund for the first time, based on an amendment of the law in 1981, and several other occupational associations subsequently followed suit. It was also extended to cover employees of medium-sized firms in this period. Those without employers, who might have paid half of the contribution, were left out until 1988–1989 when NHI eventually covered them (still under a fragmented structure). The rise of occupational members was sharper than expected, perhaps because of their attempt to escape the shadow of discrimination. In contrast, people living in the same residential area could arrange their health funds under the same 1981 amendment, although this never materialized. This was partly due to a lack of financial support from the government and partly to the absence of organisational resources. For the indigent, a Health Assistance Program was launched in 1977. It was designed to assist those receiving benefits from the Public Assistance Program, a relief scheme for the poor. The Health Assistance Program was funded by the central government (up to 80 %) and local governments (20 %).[3]

From 1988, NHI began to cover all those previously left outside of the scheme and, accordingly, became universal in scope. This was made possible by the decision of the government to pay 50 % of the contributions of regional members, which was equivalent to the contributions of employers in the case of industrial workers. This was an important move from regulator to provider in funding NHI. Underlying this policy shift was the democratization of Korean politics. The 1987 presidential election was held under a democratic constitution, and no candidate could ignore the grievances of those left outside NHI in a very competitive election. All candidates, including Roh Tae-woo—who eventually won the election—promised that NHI would cover all citizens. After this change, the state began to play the role of provider for regional members in the financing of NHI, while it maintained its role of regulator with regard to the insurance funds of various employees.

Even after NHI became universal, its health funds were managed separately in terms of collecting contributions and paying hospitals for the treatment of their members. This was a legacy of the selective approach taken when introducing NHI. The financial sustainability of health funds was of more serious concern to policymakers. At its highest point, there were 409 health funds, and their financial situation varied considerably. For example, the health fund for public employees and private schoolteachers was in good shape, as the levies were deducted directly from their salaries. Compared to this, the regional health funds, which covered informal sector workers, the self-employed, and the elderly had difficulty in collecting levies, which in turn made their financial situation precarious, despite the low spending of their members compared to other groups.

After the 1988 general election for the National Assembly, the opposition parties passed a bill to unify all health funds into one national fund, taking advantage of an unusual situation in which the opposition had more seats in total than the governing party. A national health fund would have paved the way for financial transfers among different categories of people. Industrial workers and public employees, however, made clear their strong objection to the merger of the health funds as they would lose out. In the end, this attempt was defeated by a presidential veto.

---

[3] In the case of Seoul, 50 % was financed by the local government.

5.4.3 National Pension Scheme

A National Pension Scheme (NPS) was introduced in 1988 and had the same structure of governance as NHI. The administration of this pension scheme was carried out by the National Pension Corporation, which was a quasi-governmental agency. The NPS, like NHI, began with wage earning employees in larger-scale workplaces, and steadily extended its coverage. First it covered workplaces with 10 or more employees. In 1992, it extended its coverage to workplaces with more than five employees. By 1994, it covered 27 % of the working population. In 1995, it was extended to cover farmers, fishermen, and the self-employed in rural areas. The NPS required 20-year contributions in order to be eligible for a full pension.

If one traces the historical background of the NPS, it would become clear that it was an essential part of the developmental welfare state. In 1972, President Park decided to introduce the NPS on the advice of the Korean Development Institute, a government think tank for economic policy. The idea behind it was that the NPS would mobilize domestic capital that could then be invested in social infrastructure and industry without raising the tax rate. The NPS bill was passed in the National Assembly in 1973. Eventually, however, the government had to postpone the implementation of the scheme due to a sudden rise in oil prices at the time. Nevertheless, the NPS that was introduced was almost the same as its predecessor.

Together with the Civil Service Pension Program and the Military Personnel Pension Scheme, the NPS constitutes one of the main pillars of the Korean public pension system. In this system, the mode of governance is also closer to that of regulator. As in healthcare, the government did not provide financial support for public pensions, and the public pension system is selective in its line of job categories. In relation to the Civil Service Pension Program, the government paid contributions as an employer of members of the civil service.

5.4.4 Livelihood Protection Program

The Livelihood Protection Program—a social assistance measure for the poor—was financed by state revenue, and remained strictly a means test. The level of assistance was extremely low, and recipients could not rely on this program for their living. Also, only households headed by people under 18 or over 65 years of age could receive benefits (benefits in the first category, Table 5.3). Those aged between 18 and 65 years were not entitled to public support, even though their income fell below the poverty line, which may be referred to as a demographic test. The benefits that this group of people received were healthcare and educational support for their children. There was also a third category which was eligible only for healthcare support. For this reason, only a small fraction of people officially identified as poor received any income assistance. Despite this stringent public assistance program, poverty incidence was briskly reduced during the 1960s–1970s. It came down from 40.9 % of all households in 1965 to 23.4 % in

Table 5.3   Number of people covered by public assistance programs, 1965–1990 (in thousands)

	Benefit categories			
	First	Second	Third	Percentage of total population
1965	288	72	3563	13.66
1970	306	63	2116	7.71
1975	375	52	904	3.77
1980	339	47	1500	4.96
1985	282	63	1928	5.52
1990	340	81	1835	5.26

Source National Statistical Office (1966, 1990), Suh (1981)

1970, and from 9.8 % in 1980 to 7.6 % in 1991 (Kwon and Yi 2009). This was a remarkable achievement in poverty reduction.

With the evolution of the welfare system examined above, the welfare state as a whole clearly emerged in the early 1990s with distinctive features of selective coverage and a regulatory mode of governance. In 1995, the popularly elected government introduced an Employment Insurance System, a program for unemployment insurance and training. It was the first time that Korean society recognized that unemployment was not an individual failure but a social risk worth protecting. Nevertheless, the program started only in large-scale workplaces with more than 500 employees, and with the same mode of regulatory governance.

5.5   Toward an Inclusive Developmental Welfare State

In 1997, Korea was hit by the Asian economic crisis, and extended economic growth was suddenly interrupted. A few large conglomerates, or *Chaebols*, went bankrupt while others were faced with structural adjustment. In the process, a fairly large number of people were made redundant. Many small- and medium-sized businesses also collapsed amid an unprecedented recession. Consequently, unemployment rates soared to significant levels. As the Korean economy was confronted with this severe economic crisis, it became clear that the welfare state in Korea could not cope with social challenges in an economic downturn. In particular, the welfare state was not able to tackle high unemployment, since it was based on the assumption that it could provide full employment (see Table 5.4).

During the Asian economic crisis, the longtime leader of the opposition, Kim Dae-jung, was elected to the presidency, and his government embarked on a "productive welfare" policy while undertaking neoliberal reform in the labor market. The Kim government quickly implemented social policy reforms that would enhance social protection for the vulnerable. This swift response was also related to economic restructuring. Structural reform to overcome the economic crisis would inevitably render large numbers of people unemployed. But social policy remained weak to deal with it, although the key social policy programs that had

Table 5.4 Unemployment rate in East Asia

	1996	1997	1998	1999	2000	2001	2002	2003	2004
Hong Kong	2.8	2.2	4.7	6.2	4.9	5.1	7.3	7.9	6.8
Korea	2.0	2.6	7.0	6.3	4.1	3.8	3.1	3.4	3.5
Thailand	1.1	0.9	3.4	3.0	2.4	2.6	1.8	2.2	2.1
Taiwan	2.6	2.7	2.7	2.9	3.0	4.6	5.2	5.0	4.4

Sources Asian Development Bank, Asian development outlook (2002, 2005)

started with workers were expanded beyond large-scale workplaces, and public assistance for the poor was limited, with a strict means test.

Upon assuming office, the Kim Dae-jung government carried through labor market reform, based on "social consensus." The government also set up a tripartite committee comprising representatives of business organizations, trade unions, and the government. Based on the decisions of the tripartite committee, the Korean government introduced a package of social policies to deal with unprecedented unemployment for many decades after structural adjustment. The government policy package included, among other things, a rapid extension of the Employment Insurance System, the implementation of public works projects, and the reinforcement of employment services. The Employment Insurance System, which consisted mainly of unemployment benefits and training programs, was strengthened and extended. The NPS, too, was extended to the entire community, although there remains a large section of the working population whose members are not actively paying contributions.

The government also decided to merge all health funds into a single National Health Insurance Program, which had long been Kim's policy while in opposition in 2000. A central agency, the National Health Insurance Corporation, was set up to manage the national program and administer the insurance process. Despite the merger, three separate financial accounts for public employees, industrial workers and regional members respectively were maintained for some time, because there were two ongoing issues after the merger in 2000. First, the government was not clear whether, or how, the accumulated surplus or deficit of health funds operating across the country should be merged. Second, wage earners raised doubts about the fairness of the contribution arrangements among different groups of people. With respect to wage earners, the information on remuneration was available for determining contributions, which were also directly deducted from their pay. In contrast, information on income with respect to the self-employed and informal sector workers was not readily available. Reform of the NHI alone could resolve all these issues, since it was strongly related to the country's tax system. The government was not, however, prepared to take a political risk by reforming this tax structure.

Since the merger, the National Health Insurance Corporation has developed a system of proxy measurements of the levels of income of those who belong to the category of resident-based members, that is, informal sector workers, farmers, and the self-employed. The financing of NHI has now been integrated. But the most important and immediate change that the merger of health funds brought about was the setting up of a single risk pool for health contingencies. In contrast to the previous system, all citizens belong to one national health fund. Still, the governance system remains essentially the same as before, though the government provides financial subsidies to NHI intermittently when the budget of the latter shows a deficit.

5.5.1 The Minimum Living Standard Guarantee

However, it was the MLSG that represented a clear change in the governance of the welfare state. Before the economic crisis, there were civil society groups that argued for the strengthening of social protection for the poor and vulnerable. But their efforts did not prevail before the economic crisis. During the crisis, they were able to form an advocacy coalition that actively worked toward the introduction of the MLSG. The coalition referred to Article 34 of the Constitution of the Republic of Korea, which stipulates that "All citizens are entitled to a life worthy of a human being," and to provision 5 of the same Article which specifies that "Citizens who are incapable of earning a livelihood due to a physical disability, disease, old age or other reasons shall be protected by the State..." (Lee 2000).

The Livelihood Protection Program—an early public assistance scheme, introduced in 1961 and implemented from 1965—was based on the concept of poor relief, and provided cash or in-kind support to the poor as officially defined, depending on the recipients' situation. In 1997, the number of people receiving benefits accounted for 3.1 % of the population (Ministry of Health and Welfare 2005). The level of cash benefits was estimated at half of the official poverty line, defined in absolute terms (Kwon 2001), and had a stringent means test provision. For this reason, the Livelihood Protection Program was a mere relief measure, and not sufficient to prevent people from falling below the poverty threshold. It also had a "demographic test" in which those aged between 18 and 65 years were automatically disqualified from cash benefits, as they were regarded as having earning capacity and not deserving of financial support. During the period of economic growth, a few among them managed to find sources of modest income, either from jobs or from family members or relatives. However, private incomes became harder to get since there were fewer jobs available for them, and family help did not arrive as often as before. Public works projects were intended to help these people, but could not assist all those in need. They were also temporary emergency measures which were intended to end after urgent needs had been met. In this context, the advocacy coalition argued for a new measure with wider coverage and a higher benefit level—namely, the MLSG—to replace the old public assistance program.

This proposal by the advocacy coalition was accepted by the Kim Dae-jung government, which introduced the MLSG in 2000. The MLSG aimed to address two issues: first, it was based on the idea of social rights, representing a significant change from the notion of poor relief. It also meant a modification of the concept of poverty—from poverty that was absolute to poverty that was relative. Because of the changes, those who previously did not qualify for benefits would be entitled to them, since the poverty line had risen significantly. The level of benefits was also increased because the MLSG would guarantee a living standard equal to the relative poverty line.

Second, the MLSG modified the "demographic test" and would provide benefits to those between 18 and 65 years of age if their incomes fell below the poverty level. There were, however, conditions that required these people to participate in job training programs, public works projects, or community services. In other words, certain work conditionalities were introduced. In terms of the mode of governance, the state began to assume the role of provider to an increasing degree. The financing of the program was entirely public, although the central and local governments also shared the burden. It is important to note that the Korean government employed a large number of social workers who would deal with MLSG recipients.

The year 2008 saw the introduction of Earned Income Tax Credit for near poor working families, as well as Long-term Care Insurance for the elderly. Earned Income Tax Credit—administered by the National Tax Service—is a tax-financed income support for working people whose earnings are just above the poverty line. Long-term Care Insurance is meant for the elderly, who used to be on the margins of the welfare state, and is based on social insurance principles in connection with NHI. Together with the MLSG, these provisions reflect the fact that the provider mode of governance had become increasingly significant in the Korean welfare state. The welfare state had moved toward greater inclusiveness, and was strengthened in terms of the level of welfare provision. During the global financial crisis of 2008–2009, it is fair to say that welfare programs, such as the MLSG and unemployment benefits, provided effective support. In 2009, the total welfare expenditure reached 9.56 % of gross domestic product (GDP) (Ko 2011). This was meant not only to give social protection for the unemployed and the poor during an economic crisis, but also to establish a welfare state based on the idea of citizenship.

5.6 A Universal Welfare State for the Future?

The welfare state in Korea faces considerable challenges due to the significant demographic shift toward an ageing society. In 2005, its elderly population—aged 65 years and over—reached 10.2 %, and is estimated to climb to 14 % by 2019 (National Statistical Office 2012). At the same time, the fertility rate has dropped to 1.3 %, one of the lowest in the world. The low fertility is due to a lack of social services for young families with children and has substantial implications for Korea's future economic prospects. The government has begun to increase the number of nursery places to support families with children and avert the downward spiralling of fertility rates. However, there is also a growing demand for social services for the elderly. All these will lead to a sharp rise in welfare expenditure. High unemployment among young people (7.7 % in 2011) is putting further pressure on the welfare state.

In 2011, Korean society was engaged in a social debate on welfare. For instance, university students organized a mass demonstration to demand a reduction in university fees, while politicians got into heated arguments over the decision of some local education authorities to provide free lunches to schoolchildren. Presidential hopefuls from both the governing and opposition parties also promised a universal welfare state for the future. What is interesting in this politics of welfare is that the front-running candidate of the ruling conservative party, Park Guen-hye, places her welfare commitment at the forefront of her political program. It is also a historic turn of events since she is a daughter of former President Park Chung-hee, the authoritarian leader who laid the groundwork for Korea's economic growth. Park Chung-hee's approach to development is summarized by the catchphrase "economy first and welfare later." His daughter seems to believe that it is time to bring about a welfare state in Korea, similar to the welfare states in Europe. It can be interpreted that her welfare project is a completion of her father's modernization plan. In response, the opposition party in Korea—which sees welfare as its turf—has gone further, promising free and universal healthcare, education, and care for children and the elderly. At present, it is not clear what sort of policy programs will be presented to the Korean public at the election. It is certain, however, that the welfare state in Korea—in a move toward universal welfare for its citizens—will be bigger in size and depth, and provide social protection for a wider section of its population.

Two immediate questions arise: can Korea afford a larger welfare state? And will there be notable changes in the mode of governance? The author's contention is a firm "yes." First, the size of government spending in Korea (29.3 % of GDP) is still low among countries of the Organisation for Economic Co-operation and Development (National Assembly Budget Office 2011), and revenue can be maximized by broadening the tax base and raising rates sharply. A welfare state as social investment is a cheaper option for Korea's economy of the future. Given the demographic transition and economic shift from a labor-intensive to a knowledge-intensive economy, a careful policy of welfare expansion can work as a social investment. In the context of an ageing population and low fertility, social services for families will also increase the numbers of working women and working older people. With such an investment, Korea's potential economic growth will be enhanced in the time ahead. Second, it is true that the mode of welfare governance in Korea remains largely regulatory. As discussed, this had worked while Korea tried to develop economically and, at the same time, build a welfare state. Nevertheless, with the growing size of the welfare state and the demand, especially, for universal social services, the government will inevitably assume a greater role of provider in its mix of governance.

References

Abel-Smith, B. (1994). *An introduction to health: policy, planning and financing*. London: Longman.
Asian Development Bank. (2002). *Asian development outlook*. Manila: ADB Publishing.
Asian Development Bank. (2005). *Asian development outlook*. Manila: ADB Publishing.

Cho, S., & Oh, Y. (2003). The formation of some preconditions for the condensed growth in the 1950s. *Donghyanggwa Chonmang, 59*, 258–302. (in Korean).

Ko, K. (2011). *2009 Social welfare expenditure in Korea and social policy for the disabled in comparison with the OECD countries*. Seoul: Korea Institute for Health and Social Welfare.

Kwon, H. J. (1997). Beyond European Welfare Regimes: Comparative Perspectives on East Asian Welfare Systems. *Journal of Social Policy, 26*, 467–484.

Kwon, H. J. (2001). Income transfers to the elderly in Korea and Taiwan. *Journal of Social Policy, 30*, 81–93.

Kwon, H. J. (2005). Transforming the developmental welfare state in East Asia. *Development and Change, 36*, 477–497.

Kwon, H. J., & Yi, I. (2009). Economic development and poverty reduction in Korea: governing multifunctional institutions. *Development and Change, 40*, 769–792.

Lee, H. (2000). *A comparative analysis of participants in policy making: Kim Young-sam and Kim Dae-jung governments*. Seoul (in Korean): Sung Kyun Kwan University.

Mills, A. (1985). Economic aspect of health insurance. In A. Mills & K. Lee (Eds.), *The economics of health insurance in developing countries*. Oxford: Oxford University Press.

Ministry of Health and Welfare. (2005). *Yearbook of health and statistics*. Seoul: MoHW.

National Assembly Budget Office. (2011). *Republic of Korea's 2009 budget*. Seoul: National Assembly Budget Office.

National Health Insurance Agency. (1990). *National health insurance statistical yearbook*. Seoul: National Health Insurance Agency.

National Statistical Office. (1966). *Korea statistical yearbook*. Seoul: Economic Planning Board.

National Statistical Office. (1990). *Korea statistical yearbook*. Seoul: Ministry of Strategy and Finance.

National Statistical Office. (2012). *Population projection by proivince: 2010–2040*. Daejeon: National Statistical Office. (in Korean).

Park, C. K. (1979). *Health financing and health insurance in Korea*, vol. (in Korean). Seoul: KDI.

Ringen, S., Kwon, H., Yi, I., Kim, T., & Lee, J. (2011). *The Korean state and social policy: How south Korea lifted itself from poverty and dictatorship to affluence and democracy*. New York: Oxford University Press.

Sin, P. (1988). Comparative research on land refrom in Korea and Taiwan. *Korea and World Politics, 4*(2) (in Korean).

Suh, S.–M. et al. (1981). *The situation of poverty and policies for the poor*. Seoul: Korea Development Institute. (in Korean).

Woo, J. (1991). *Race to the Swift: State and Finance in Korean Industrialization*. New York: Columbia University Press.

Yi, I. (2007). *The Politics of Occupational Welfare in Korea*. Fukuoka: Hana-Syoin.

Chapter 6
Trade Policy for Development: Paradigm Shift from Mercantilism to Liberalism

Min Gyo Koo

6.1 Introduction

At the end of 2011, the Republic of Korea (hereinafter Korea) became the ninth country to join the "one-trillion-dollar trading club," departing from the ranks of newly emerging countries to join the ranks of trade giants. After reaching the $100 million mark in 1964, Korea's exports grew more than five thousand times in 47 years, making it the seventh-largest exporting country in the world. Its economic development model has been characterized as export-oriented industrialization (EOI). In trade policy terms, Korea has adopted a mercantilist policy centered on export promotion and import protection, which traces back to its developmental period in the early 1960s. For the past two decades, however, Korea's trade policy has undergone a fundamental transformation as a result of democratization and globalization. The departure from its traditional mercantilist policy can be best illustrated by its active pursuit of free trade agreements (FTAs). This trend took its most pronounced turn when Korea concluded an FTA with the world's largest economy, the United States (US), in 2007. The global economic crisis in 2008 has not reduced the speed and scope of Korea's FTA initiative, as demonstrated by the conclusion of agreements with India in 2009 and the European Union (EU) in 2010.

In an era of maturing democracy, the rapidly changing electoral and legislative dynamics have structured Korea's trade policy options. Underlying the structured choices are the difficult challenges confronting policymakers who now have to

---

This chapter is adapted from, and draws heavily on, the author's previous publications as cited in the references section.

M. G. Koo (✉)
Graduate School of Public Administration, Seoul National University, Seoul 151-742, Republic of Korea
e-mail: mgkoo@snu.ac.kr

satisfy not only domestic constituents, but also international communities, including foreign governments, multinational firms, and international organizations. Against this backdrop, this chapter aims to answer four basic questions: What factors have contributed to the successful evolution of Korea's trade policy? How have government institutions impacted the way in which Korea has responded to policy opportunities and challenges in trade issue areas? How do electoral and legislative politics interact with Korea's new trade policy strategy, which seeks to strike a right balance between neodevelopmentalism and neoliberalism? And how do institutional configurations of domestic political players and the structure of international bargaining affect eventual policy choices?

From an analytical point of view, the significance of Korea's new trade policy initiative is threefold. First, it constitutes a notable shift toward liberalism, departing from a mercantilist approach characterized by a policy mix of import protection and export promotion. Second, it has been shaped by a top-down political initiative rather than a bottom-up demand from business groups and the general public. And third, despite Korea's liberal but state-centric nature, its partisan politics has led its trade policy to be closely embedded in the country's social fabric, both competitive and noncompetitive.

It would be preposterous to argue that Korean policy elites have embraced new trade policy initiatives as a tool to promote purely neoliberal economic goals in a political vacuum. In particular, the country's FTA policy is hardly insulated from societal pressures and electoral politics. Korea's policy elites have made no secret of the fact that they intend to use FTAs to improve their country's industrial and economic competitiveness. At the same time, generous side payments to those who may be disadvantaged by greater trade openness aptly illustrate the manner in which partisan politics has structured the dynamics between state elites and protectionist veto players, thus resulting in a new policy equilibrium between liberalization and social protection.

The remainder of this chapter unfolds as follows. Section 6.2 outlines the origins of Korea's mercantilist trade policy from a historical and institutional perspective. Section 6.3 analyzes the transformation of the country's trade policy in an era of democratization and globalization. It also demonstrates that generous compensation measures designed for potential losers of free trade have been an outcome of Korea's unique partisan politics, which has structured the dynamics between trade policy elites and affected interest groups. Section 6.4 summarizes the key arguments and draws policy implications for developing countries, most of which face the twin challenges of democratization and globalization.

6.2 Origins of Korea's Mercantilist Trade Policy

Korea's mercantilist trade policy traces back to its developmental period that started in the early 1960s. In May 1961, a military coup led by General Park Chung-hee overthrew the fledgling democratic regime that had replaced Syngman

Rhee's in the previous year. President Park felt a strong urge to improve his country's economic relations with Japan and the US. He realized he could no longer delay negotiations for normalizing Korea's relations with Japan and, in October 1962, sent his right-hand man, Kim Jong-pil—director of the Korean Central Intelligence Agency—to Tokyo as chief negotiator to conclude the prolonged discussions. To be sure, the path to a final agreement was not an easy one. In their second meeting in November, Kim and his Japanese counterpart, Foreign Minister Masayoshi Ohira, reached a secret agreement on the amount of a financial reparations package.[1]

The 1962 Kim-Ohira secret agreement was a breakthrough in the stalemated talks, but left many problems. The diplomatic atmosphere between Korea and Japan became dangerously charged with mutual suspicion when the Kim-Ohira memorandum was released in January 1963. In Korea, the secretive manner in which Kim had handled the issue sparked public fear of a national sellout in return for Japan's economic aid or "gift for Korean independence," instead of "reparations" for Japan's past atrocities. The revelation touched off Korean nationalism, leading to nationwide demonstrations against normalization talks (Koo 2009a, p. 74).

President Park had to contend with the public's growing sense of indignation. He sent Kim again in March 1964 to Tokyo as presidential envoy to resume the stalemated talks. The announcement in Tokyo that a draft treaty was imminent drew allegations in Korea that Kim had secretly cut another deal with his Japanese counterpart by conceding Korea's negotiating position in exchange for a vast amount of Japanese funds for his own profit and the ruling party's coffers. Although Park removed Kim in the middle of the Tokyo negotiations, domestic protests continued to attack Kim's association with widespread corruption in the ruling Democratic Republican Party (DRP), in which Kim held the party chairmanship. In addition, factions developed within the ruling party between pro- and anti-Kim forces, threatening the stability of the entire government. The turmoil resulted in Kim's resignation from the DRP chairmanship in June 1964 and his departure for the US on an extended leave of absence (Lee 1990, pp. 169–170; Lee 1995a, b, pp. 200–201; Cha 1996, p. 135).

Despite the complex domestic power dynamics, geopolitical conditions began to change dramatically toward a Korean-Japanese rapprochement. It is widely held that the US created the necessary momentum for concluding a normalization treaty in 1965. Until 1963, the US maintained a somewhat indifferent position toward the normalization talks. While reconciliation between Seoul and Tokyo would be beneficial to American security interests in the region, the issue did not have a high priority in Washington, except among regional experts. By 1964, however,

---

[1] The Kim-Ohira memorandum states that Japan would pay $300 million in grants over the following 10 years; it would loan a further $200 million—also over a period of 10 years—from its Overseas Economic Cooperation Fund, with a repayment schedule of 20 years at 3.5 % interest, deferred for 7 years; and that it would arrange for private loans of over $100 million through its Export–Import Bank (Lee 1995a, b, pp. 124–125).

increasingly intense Cold War competition in East Asia prompted a significant change in the US approach.[2] In face of growing regional uncertainties, a stable relationship between America's two major allies, Korea and Japan, became the highest concern. The US began to push strongly for a conclusion of the prolonged normalization negotiations. America's hegemonic position certainly assured that potential bilateral tensions between Korea and Japan took place within certain confines. It was no coincidence that US President Lyndon Johnson reiterated his unconditional backing for a Korea-Japan settlement and its importance not only for the two countries, but also for the anti-communist front in East Asia. Johnson also confirmed in conversations with Park that American military and economic assistance to Korea would remain intact after normalization (Lee 1995a, b, pp. 249–50, 351–52; Cha 1996, pp. 131–135, 141).

Aside from the realities of the Cold War containment network and the overriding demands of alliance politics, the high priority given to a stable economic relationship motivated both Korea and Japan to normalize their bilateral relations. In particular, the Park government faced a near-desperate situation as the first 5-year development plan (1962–1966) failed to overcome the persistent economic troubles of poverty and low levels of development. A steady decline in US economic aid further exacerbated the grim situation, as it reached a 16-year low in 1965. President Park decided to "live or die" with the normalization issue. Korea's *chaebol* also lobbied strongly for normalization. Especially, appealing to these groups was the prospect of acquiring Japanese technology and manufacturing capabilities in industries vacated by Japan's ascension up the product cycle. In government white papers for 1965 and numerous public statements, the Park administration stressed a pragmatic need to overcome historical animosities and normalize ties with Japan (Lee 1990, pp. 170–171; Cha 1996, pp. 128–129).[3]

---

[2] In the early 1960s, the Chinese communist threat loomed large. Beijing's geopolitical divorce from Moscow, its signing of a mutual defense treaty with North Korea (1961), and its support for Southeast Asian communist movements strongly indicated to US policymakers that an Asian communist front was being consolidated. China's successful nuclear tests—in October 1964 and May 1965—coincided with its aggressive rhetoric on Taiwan, further exacerbating threat perceptions in the rest of the region. The security outlook in Southeast Asia appeared even less promising. In April 1965, US commitment to a deteriorating situation in Indochina became much more complicated with the decision to send American troops to the conflict (Cha 1996, pp. 131–142).

[3] In Japan, political elites were aware of their strengths concerning Korea's desperate economic needs. Prime Minister Eisaku Sato and the elder Liberal Democratic Party politicians, particularly former Prime Minister Nobusuke Kishi, decided to take full advantage of a strong but relatively pro-Japan Korean dictator to accelerate the negotiation process (Lee 1990, pp. 169–170). Voices within the Korean Ministry of Foreign Affairs (MOFA) also pressed strongly for a settlement. As a 1965 MOFA white paper noted, the reestablishment of ties with Korea was a "historical inevitability" and Park's urgent need for foreign capital and political legitimacy offered relatively low cost for a normalization agreement with Korea. The Sato government faced additional pressure from the powerful Japanese business lobby. Korea was becoming an increasingly important export market for Japan. Park's second 5-year plan (1967–1971) would offer Japanese firms a plethora of large-scale projects, all of which could be underwritten by the financial package to be followed by a normalization settlement (Bridges 1993, pp. 32–33; Cha 1996, pp. 129–130).

Foreign Ministers Etsusaburo Shiina and Lee Dong-won finally signed the Treaty on Basic Relations and four other agreements in Tokyo on June 22, 1965. The normalization treaty provided a fledgling Korean economy with much-needed foreign capital: An $845 million package of government and commercial loans, grants-in-aid, and property claims. The treaty also cleared the way for an extensive expansion of trade relations that helped Japan to surpass the US as Korea's foremost trading partner within just a year. As its market grew, Korea became increasingly important to Japan as an importer of greater quantities of Japanese goods (Cha 1996, pp. 124). During the period 1961–1965, Korea's exports to Japan rose from $19 million to $44 million, while its imports climbed from $69 million to $167 million. As a result, Korea's trade dependence on Japan as a share of its gross domestic product (GDP) jumped from 3.77 to 6.98 %. Although the conclusion of the normalization treaty stood on somewhat shaky ground, it was certainly a big step forward toward the restoration of amicable relations. In addition to the overriding demands of alliance politics at the height of the Cold War, the high priority given to a stable economic relationship motivated both Korea and Japan to make the conscious choice to normalize their diplomatic relations (Koo 2009a, pp. 77–78).

Korea's dramatic economic takeoff resulted from its export-oriented industrialization, together with heavy protectionism under the auspices of America's Cold War strategy. Following in the footsteps of the Japanese developmental model, Korea's active promotion of the export sector allowed this once reclusive country to aggressively participate in the global market. As a trade-dependent nation, Korea's full integration into the world trading system was not a matter of choice but of survival (Koo 2006, pp. 142–143). As shown in Table 6.1, its GDP grew at an average annual rate of 8.8 % during the period 1965–1979, while its international trade increased almost 60-fold for the same period. It is also notable that Korea's total trade as a share of GDP has become more than 50 % since 1973.

In the political vacuum left by the assassination of President Park in October 1979, General Chun Doo-hwan (1980–1988) seized power through a military coup, overthrowing the interim government in December 1979, and getting himself elected president in August 1980. President Chun and his successor, Roh Tae-woo (1988–1993), continued with the EOI strategy. In the 1980s, Korean GDP grew rapidly at an average annual rate of 8.7 %. In particular, the 3-year period from 1986 to 1988 witnessed an unprecedented economic boom, with an average GDP growth rate of 10.8 % because of the so-called "three lows"—a low yen, a low exchange rate, and low oil prices. Korea experienced trade surpluses for the first time with a 3-year total of $18 billion. Its trade dependence on Japan remained significantly in double digits throughout the 1980s, although its trade deficit with Japan fell from a peak of $5.4 billion in 1986 to $3.8 billion in 1988. Deeper bilateral economic relations were reinforced by the rise of government aid and foreign direct investment, particularly after the 1985 Plaza Accord that pushed the value of the yen to nearly twice its value against the US dollar (Bridges 1993, 102–103).

Table 6.1 Korea's economic outlook, 1961–1997

Year	Population (million)	GDP (current US$ billion)	Annual GDP growth rate (percent)	Export (current US$ million)	Import (current US$ million)	Total trade (exports plus imports, current US$ million)	Share of total trade in GDP (%)
1961	25.7	2.4	4.94	38	297	335	14.2
1962	26.4	2.7	2.46	55	415	470	17.1
1963	27.1	3.9	9.53	86	558	644	16.7
1964	27.8	3.4	7.56	117	403	520	15.5
1965	28.5	3.0	5.19	171	454	625	20.7
1966	29.2	3.8	12.70	249	716	965	25.4
1967	29.9	4.7	6.10	319	996	1,315	28.0
1968	30.6	6.0	11.70	455	1,468	1,923	32.3
1969	31.2	7.5	14.10	624	1,823	2,447	32.7
1970	31.9	8.9	8.34	844	1,984	2,828	31.8
1971	32.6	9.9	8.24	1,079	2,394	3,473	35.3
1972	33.3	10.7	4.47	1,631	2,522	4,153	38.7
1973	33.9	13.7	12.03	3,254	4,240	7,494	54.7
1974	34.6	19.2	7.18	4,508	6,852	11,360	59.1
1975	35.3	21.5	5.95	5,110	7,274	12,384	57.7
1976	35.8	29.6	10.57	7,715	8,694	16,409	55.5
1977	36.4	37.9	9.99	10,048	10,806	20,854	55.0
1978	37.0	51.1	9.30	12,594	14,975	27,569	53.9
1979	37.5	65.6	6.78	15,036	20,176	35,212	53.7
1980	38.1	63.8	−1.49	17,439	22,063	39,502	61.9
1981	38.7	71.5	6.16	21,271	26,154	47,425	66.4
1982	39.3	76.2	7.33	21,827	24,250	46,077	60.5
1983	39.9	84.5	10.77	24,459	26,196	50,655	59.9
1984	40.4	93.2	8.10	29,259	30,628	59,887	64.2
1985	40.8	96.6	6.80	30,289	31,058	61,347	63.5
1986	41.2	111.3	10.62	34,793	31,734	66,527	59.8
1987	41.6	140.0	11.10	47,303	41,026	88,329	63.1
1988	42.0	187.4	10.64	60,683	51,812	112,495	60.0
1989	42.4	230.5	6.74	60,496	60,210	120,706	52.4
1990	42.9	263.8	9.16	65,021	69,858	134,879	51.1
1991	43.3	308.2	9.39	71,875	81,508	153,383	49.8
1992	43.7	329.9	5.88	76,641	81,777	158,418	48.0
1993	44.1	362.1	6.13	81,736	83,800	165,536	45.7
1994	44.5	423.4	8.54	96,040	102,348	198,388	46.9
1995	45.1	517.1	9.17	131,312	135,110	266,422	51.5
1996	45.5	557.6	7.00	137,413	150,157	287,570	51.6
1997	46.0	516.3	4.65	144,023	144,634	288,657	55.9

Sources International Monetary Fund; World Bank

The story of Korea's successful EOI, often dubbed the "miracle on the Han River," is a good example of developmental mercantilism.[4] The institutional marriage of developmentalism and mercantilism quickly spread throughout the country, brokered by the social embeddedness of industrial and trade policies.[5] The Korean developmental state successfully managed to industrialize and expand the national economy at a pace that could attract almost all economically motivated citizens. Its policy focus was on creating jobs and improving incomes as rapidly as possible.

Yet Korea's EOI clearly lacked the comprehensive social security system found in the West (Chang 2007, p. 67). As elsewhere in the world, Korea's societal interests have been divided along sectoral lines between competitive and uncompetitive industries, while the relative scarcity of land has made the urban–rural divide a permanent feature of the country's political economy. Although the Korean government made some efforts to establish a comprehensive social protection system, its social welfare policies predominantly consisted of social insurance programs; people were required to pay contributions prior to entitlement to social benefits. As a result, only those who had formal employment had access to social protection, leaving those who were self-employed, or informally employed, outside the system. The social policies in the early developmental period were geared toward economic development and covered only a narrow section of the population. Against this background, Korea's developmental state provided minimum safeguards for uncompetitive sectors and rural areas through multilayered formal and informal trade barriers, although they were largely exploited in favor of competitive, export-oriented sectors and urban areas (Kwon 2005).[6]

With the advent of civilian rule in 1993, traditionally disadvantaged groups became better organized and more vocal, thus making it even harder for the government to negotiate free trade deals that would adversely affect uncompetitive and import-competing industries. During the Uruguay Round (UR) of trade talks, for instance, the Korean government made desperate efforts to protect rice and other

---

[4] In his analysis of the regime shift in Japan, T. J. Pempel demonstrated that public policies of "embedded mercantilism" were pursued in the 1960s to promote macroeconomic success—budgets were typically balanced, inflation was held low, and any corporatist bargaining took place at the corporate, not the national, level. From this perspective, the political tensions that had divided postwar Japan were substantially reduced, not through Keynesianism, inflation, or corporatism, but through rapid growth that relied on domestic protection, industrial policy, and export promotion. The resultant conservative regime that emerged in Japan in the 1960s looked distinctly different from those of other advanced industrialized democracies (Pempel 1998, pp. 5–10).

[5] East Asia scholars tend to use the term "embeddedness" in a proactive manner. They argue that, when combined with the autonomous developmental states, embeddedness allows states to go beyond being welfare states, as defined by the traditional "embedded liberalism" literature. In this respect, "developmental mercantilism" is closely associated with "embedded mercantilism." For more discussions about Korea's developmental state, see Amsden (1989) and Woo-Cumings (1999).

[6] For more details about the evolution of Korea's welfare state, see the chapter by Kwon in this volume.

agricultural and fishery products at the expense of consumers and of Korea's international reputation as a free trading country. The relatively short history of Korea's industrialization since the 1970s means that many Koreans continue to have rural roots, despite large-scale migration to urban areas. Before the UR negotiation, agriculture had been completely excluded from the free trade debate. Although Korea had to agree to open its agricultural market under the UR agreement, its sensitive agricultural sectors, such as rice and dairy, remained largely outside the global competition.[7]

6.3 Globalization and Institutional Transformation

The political and economic conditions, both external and internal, that underpinned Korea's traditional trade policy paradigm came under heavy pressure at the end of the 1990s. Most importantly, the outbreak of the Asian financial crisis of 1997–1998 shattered the illusion of Korea's unstoppable economic growth, thus having a profound impact on the way in which the country perceived its economic survival in a world of deeper and wider globalization.[8]

As with many other East Asian countries, Korea began to hold the perception of being pushed away by the Washington Consensus, which aggressively promoted the policies of deregulation, privatization, and liberalization as prerequisites for economic development (Dieter 2009, p. 76). Although the International Monetary Fund (IMF) loan package caused a region-wide resentment of the Washington-dominated agency, Korea and other crisis-ridden countries in the region had little choice.[9] In addition, the 1999 World Trade Organization (WTO) Ministerial Conference in Seattle failed to launch a new round of trade talks, leading Korea's top policymakers to recognize that the mediocre performance of the WTO, and

---

[7] Under the UR agreement, Korea received a 10-year exception to tariffication of rice imports in return for establishing a minimum market access (MMA) quota. Under this quota, Korea's rice imports grew over 10 years from 0 to 4 % of domestic consumption during the base period. The Korean government, through state trading enterprises, exercised full control over the purchase, distribution, and end use of imported rice. The original MMA arrangement expired at the end of 2004, but Korea successfully negotiated a 10-year extension. It also established tariff-rate quotas that were intended to provide minimum access to previously closed markets or to maintain pre-UR access (Office of the United States Trade Representative 2006).

[8] Kim (2011) argues that Korea has pursued a "bandwagoning" strategy, "putting too much emphasis on accepting and adapting to neoliberal globalization," and that it now "needs to pursue a more flexible national strategy to deal with multiple types of globalization."

[9] According to Fred Bergsten (2000, p. 22), "most East Asians feel that they were both let down and put upon by the West in the crisis." They believe that the West, in particular the US, "let down" Asia because Western financial institutions and other actors caused or exacerbated the crisis by withdrawing their money from the region and then refused, as did the US, to take part in rescue operations to manage it. They believe that East Asia has been "put upon" by the West because of the way in which, through the IMF, the West dictated the international response to the crisis and because of the perceived consequences of the IMF's prescriptions. See also Pempel (1999) and Wade (2000).

increasing competition in its traditional export markets, could hurt export-dependent Korea (Cheong 1999; Sohn 2001).

In the immediate aftermath of the Asian financial crisis, Korea's protectionist veto players, such as labor unions and farmers' organizations, were temporarily disorganized due to the liberal reform of President Kim Dae-jung (1998–2003) and the austerity program imposed by the IMF (Chang 2007, p. 69). Although some farmers' groups and labor unions remained militant, their political influence eroded significantly, as both their absolute and relative shares in the economy continued to decline.[10] It became clear that developmental mercantilism alone was not able to cope with the unprecedented economic hardships.

In response to the financial and economic turmoil, the Kim government implemented the so-called IMF reforms, dramatically altering Korea's development path. The case of import diversification rules illustrates this point. In trying to correct the worsening trade deficit with Japan, the Korean government restricted or completely excluded certain Japanese products from the Korean market.[11] The problem for the Korean government was to balance the needs of its own industries for key components and products from Japan against its fears that the Japanese would dominate certain sectors of the domestic market if allowed complete freedom. The Japanese government protested regularly about these restrictions, which it regarded as a violation of the principles of the General Agreement on Tariffs and Trade prohibiting quantitative restrictions, but did nothing to retaliate, since—in practice—Japanese companies were able to find ways around these restrictions (Bridges 1993, pp. 95–96). This protectionist practice was gradually phased out at the end of the 1990s as a result of the rescue loan package agreement between Korea and the IMF. Apparently, the elimination of the import diversification rules was influenced by Japan, which was one of the principal patrons of the IMF rescue package for Korea (Koo 2009a, p. 81).

As shown in Table 6.2, Korea's trade strength quickly bounced back after the financial crisis and has grown even more rapidly since then. The average share of trade in GDP grew from 52 % (1987–1996) to 68.6 % (1999–2010). Despite brief hiccups due to the 2008 global economic crisis, the rising trend continues, making Korea the seventh-largest exporter as of 2011. Korea owes this remarkable recovery from the Asian financial crisis to the transformation of its trade strategy.

---

[10] The share of agriculture, forestry, and fisheries in Korea's total employment decreased continuously from 17.9 % in 1990 to 8.1 % in 2004. The share of the three sectors in Korea's GDP was less than 4 % in 2003 (Ministry of Finance and Economy 2005).

[11] Under a 1977 government directive to diversify imports, 50 products from Southeast Asian countries were subjected to import approval. Japan was not specifically designated, but was the implied target. In 1980, the list was expanded, and formal restrictions were applied to the country—that is, Japan—which had been the largest exporter to Korea in the previous year. When, in 1982, Saudi Arabia became the largest source of imports, this qualification was changed to include the largest source of imports over the previous 5 years. The list has fluctuated in length, from 162 Japanese products subject to this system in July 1982, to a peak of 344 items in April 1988, before falling to 258 in 1991. This list was regularly amended.

Table 6.2 Korea's economic outlook, 1998–2010

Year	Population (million)	GDP (current US$ billion)	Annual GDP growth rate (%)	Export (current US$ billion)	Import (current US$ billion)	Total trade (exports plus imports, current US$ million)	Share of total trade in GDP (%)
1998	46.3	345.4	−6.85	132.7	93.4	226.1	65.4
1999	46.6	445.4	9.49	143.9	119.7	263.6	59.2
2000	47.0	533.4	8.49	172.3	160.5	332.8	62.4
2001	47.4	504.6	3.97	150.4	141.1	291.5	57.8
2002	47.6	575.9	7.15	162.3	152.1	314.4	54.6
2003	47.9	643.8	2.80	193.8	178.8	372.6	57.9
2004	48.0	722.0	4.62	254.4	224.5	478.9	66.3
2005	48.1	844.9	3.96	285.5	261.2	546.7	64.7
2006	48.4	951.8	5.18	326.3	309.4	635.7	66.8
2007	48.6	1,049.2	5.11	373.7	356.8	730.5	69.6
2008	48.9	931.4	2.30	426.8	435.3	862.1	92.6
2009	49.2	834.1	0.32	373.2	323.1	696.3	83.5
2010	49.4	1,014.9	6.32	471.1	425.3	896.4	88.3

Sources International Monetary Fund; World Bank

Some scholars believe that the economic reforms under Kim led to the demise of "Korea, Inc.," the symbiotic relationship between government and business that was at the heart of the country's developmental state (Lee and Han 2006). Even with changes, however, the reform process reflected the legacies of the developmental state, with the state continuing to play an important role in planning, implementing, and sustaining economic reforms (Lim 2010). Under President Kim's strong executive power and public support for liberal restructuring, the new FTA initiative went unchallenged, if not unnoticed, by traditional protectionist interests. The Kim government took the initiative in shifting Korea's policy away from its earlier focus on access to the US market through global multilateralism and the protection of uncompetitive domestic industries (Koo 2009b, pp. 186–188). In November 1998, the government's Inter-Ministerial Trade Policy Coordination Committee announced that Korea would start FTA negotiations with Chile, while conducting feasibility studies with other prospective FTA partners such as the US, Japan, New Zealand, and Thailand (Sohn 2001).

Although the link between the FTAs and domestic reform was not clearly defined, Kim's FTA policy was designed as a liberal strategy to address the dire need for economic liberalization under the growing pressure of globalization. This liberal shift of the state was an integral part of its resuscitated developmentalism, focusing on export industries. The Kim administration wanted to ensure the survival of most of Korea's major export firms, but at the same time clearly understood that post-crisis external conditions would not allow Korea to free ride on others' markets any longer. It was indeed the beginning of an irreversible transformation of the country's trade policy paradigm (Koo 2010).

The policy shift toward FTAs under President Kim did mark a dramatic departure from Korea's developmental mercantilist policy. Yet it was not until President Roh entered office in 2003 that the comprehensive road map for FTAs and detailed action plans for its multitrack FTA strategy was completed (Lee 2006; Ministry of Foreign Affairs and Trade 2006). In contrast to its rather peripheral position on President Kim's economic and strategic agenda, the FTA policy became a core element of President Roh's economic policy reform and regionalist vision. At first glance, it appears that Roh reluctantly inherited his predecessor Kim's economic policy agenda because the former's principal power base included those who were negatively affected by trade liberalization. Looked at beneath the surface, however, Roh further expanded it by completing a road map for Korea's multitrack FTAs and adopting comprehensive side payments to adversely affected groups (Koo 2010).

The nature and scope of Korea's shift in trade policy focus under Roh is best illustrated by the Korea-United States (KORUS) FTA negotiations. Initially, the Roh administration's move toward the KORUS FTA came as a surprise because, according to its original FTA road map, a comprehensive FTA with a large economy like the US was a long-term goal, while deals with lighter trading partners such as Chile, Mexico, and Canada had top priority. This change in the sequence of FTA partner selection meant an implicit but noticeable emphasis on strategic value in Korea's FTA equations. Certainly, Korea expected generous economic gains from an FTA with the US. Its top policy elites believed that an FTA with the US would accelerate Korea's market-oriented reform process and upgrade its economy, thus helping overcome the likely scenario of a Korea "sandwiched" between Japan and China.[12] On this score, Korea's then trade minister, Kim Hyun-chong, was particularly enthusiastic. He made no secret of the fact that the KORUS FTA would be an effective means to transform the structure of the Korean economy, departing from its replication of the Japanese developmental model and adopting an American-style liberal economy.[13]

Ultimately, President Roh made the final decision. He became a champion of the FTA as a diplomatic tool to strengthen strategic ties with the US. President Roh supported Minister Kim's ambitious idea at the expense of his loyal constituents, including progressive civil groups, labor unions, and farmers' associations. He clearly understood the strategic utility of the FTA. Equally important was the fact that Roh became a true believer in free trade and the opening of markets as a key to economic growth.[14] This was in stark contrast to his supposedly anti-American, populist background. Amidst the controversy over the costs and benefits of the KORUS FTA, he publicly identified himself as a "leftist liberal"—leftist because he desired a self-reliant, nation-first (*minzok useon*) Korea, and liberal because he believed in the power

---

[12] In a speech to the Korean Chamber of Commerce and Industry on March 28, 2006, President Roh asserted: "China is surging. Japan is reviving. Trapped between China and Japan, Korea desperately needs to develop a strategy to cope with current challenges. One of the most effective ways to accomplish this goal is to improve our country's competitive edge against China and Japan in the US market by concluding a KORUS FTA" (quoted in Koo 2009b, p. 190).

[13] Interview with Minister Kim Hyun-chong, May 2009 (quoted in Sohn and Koo 2011, p. 443).

[14] Interview with Minister Kim Hyun-chong, May 2009 (quoted in Sohn and Koo 2011, p. 450).

of free trade.[15] More notably, he rejected the Japanese "flying geese" model of development,[16] saying that it had already outlived its utility for Korea. His assertion, instead, was that Korea should find its economic future in high-technology and service industries, moving away from the traditional focus on heavy manufacturing. Economic nationalism was critical to the rise of the developmental state approach in Korea, although this time it took the form of liberalism rather than mercantilism.

Institutionally, the empowerment of the Office of the Minister for Trade (OMT) demonstrated renewed enthusiasm and commitment under Roh as the once beleaguered institution took firm root within the government with its mandate to initiate and negotiate FTAs.[17] As a champion of liberal economic ideas, the OMT was relatively insulated from pressure from special interest groups, which in turn prevents it from obtaining sufficient public support for FTAs.[18] Nevertheless, the top-down nature of Korea's FTA initiative, as promoted by the OMT, indicates that its FTA strategy is inherently developmentalist in tone and scope. In addition, its liberal leanings notwithstanding, Roh's FTA strategy in fact built upon the long-standing embeddedness of the state (Koo 2010).[19]

Under these circumstances, it is not surprising that Korea's uncompetitive sectors felt more victimized by their government's FTA initiatives with potentially stronger liberal overtones. For those skeptics, the government's effort to restructure the

[15] On February 5, 2008, in a forum arranged on the fifth anniversary of his inauguration, Roh argued: "Some label me as leftist, others liberal. What is important is adopting necessary policies for our economy. In that sense, my government could be called leftist liberals" (quoted in Sohn and Koo 2011, p. 450).

[16] The concept of "flying geese" was first used by the Japanese economist Kaname Akamatsu (1937). Akamatsu found that the process of industrialization in the Japanese empire in the 1920s–1930s followed three stages: import of new products, import substitution, and export. This process appeared as an inverse "V" shape, resembling the flight pattern of wild geese migrating between Japan and Siberia. Akamatsu's product cycle theory was used to justify the hierarchically organized division of labor in the Greater East Asia Co-Prosperity Sphere. Subsequent adherents of the flying geese model—Korea and Taiwan in the 1960s, and later developers Thailand, Malaysia, and Indonesia in the 1990s—grew rapidly as a result of technology and process transfer through the investment and outsourcing of Japanese companies, as these companies followed low-cost production in the later stages of product cycles (Yamazawa 1990).

[17] As a result of the 1998 government organization reforms, which were intended to consolidate institutional support for President Kim's reform agenda, the OMT was formed under the Ministry of Foreign Affairs and Trade (Koo 2006, p. 148). However, the OMT was abolished and its trade negotiating power has been delegated to the Ministry of Industry, Trade and Energy as a result of the 2013 government organization reforms.

[18] The OMT's neoliberal policy orientation was further highlighted by the appointment of its third trade minister, Kim Hyun-chong, in July 2004, as well as the promotion of its first trade minister, Han Duk-soo (1998–2004), to the post of deputy prime minister and minister of finance and economy. For the critics of neoliberal economic policy as well as hard core Korean nationalists, Trade Minister Kim was a bad choice, not only because he advocated neoliberal economic policies, but also because he grew up in the US and was trained there as a lawyer, which—the critics argued—undermined his nationalist credentials (Koo 2009b, p. 189).

[19] In many respects, the institutional design and operation of the OMT on trade issues resembled the Economic Planning Board (EPB) in broader economic policy areas during 1960s–1980s. For more details about the way in which the EPB managed and coordinated Korea's economic policy, see Choi's chapter in this volume.

economy by inviting external pressure—the FTAs—could only worsen the economic polarization in Korea, rather than providing an opportunity to upgrade its economy to a more advanced level (Lee 2006, p. 6). The debate surrounding the KORUS FTA illustrated this point. In contrast to their temporary disorganization during the Kim Dae-jung period, traditional protectionist groups under Roh Moo-hyun recovered from the shadow of the financial crisis and began to work closely with anti-globalization non-governmental organizations and anti-capital labor unions. Some radicals even dubbed the implicit linkage of the KORUS FTA to neoliberal reforms "the second IMF-imposed liberalization" (National Emergency Conference 2007). This observation confirmed findings in the broader literature on post-crisis economic reform in Korea.[20]

As a result, the Roh administration was forced to combine generous side payments with its market opening commitments in order to cushion citizens from the vagaries of the international economy in return for public support for openness. Roh pledged many FTA-related side payments. For instance, the ratification of the Korea-Chile FTA in February 2004 was followed by the passage of a special law designed to make up for its potential financial damage to the farming and fishing industries. Despite criticism of the government's excessive financial commitment to declining sectors, over $80 billion of public and private funds were earmarked for rescue programs for the farming and fishing sectors over a 10-year period (Ministry of Foreign Affairs and Trade 2004). Other examples include a series of pledged side payments in the form of government subsidies and grants-in-aid during the KORUS FTA negotiations. In March 2006, the Roh government pledged to provide the Korean movie industry with a government funds amounting to $400 million as compensation for cutting Korea's annual screen quota in favor of the US.[21] The Roh government also committed itself to providing cash allowances for 7 years to offset income losses of up to 85 % for farmers and fishermen once the KORUS FTA went into effect. Aside from this, Korean farmers and fishermen were to receive government subsidies for 5 years if they went out of business due to the KORUS FTA.[22]

The conservative Lee Myung-bak administration (2008–2013) made a dramatic break with the progressive policies of the preceding decade, with the FTA strategy being one of the few areas in which it followed in the footsteps of its predecessors.

---

[20] For instance, Lim (2010) found that the relationship among politicians, bureaucrats, and interest groups have been altered, so that the relative power of interest groups has been strengthened vis-à-vis politicians and bureaucrats in the fields of manufacturing, information technology, and finance.

[21] Korea's screen quota system was designed to stem a flood of Hollywood blockbusters. Korea originally had a quota of 146 days or 40 % reserved for domestic films; this was cut to 73 days or 20 % starting July 1, 2006 (Chosun Ilbo 2006a, b).

[22] To boost investment in agriculture, the Roh government promised to encourage the creation of private agricultural investment funds, with agriculture-related companies being allowed to bring in chief executive officers from outside the industry. The government would offer low-interest loans to businesses that lost more than 25 % of their sales due to the KORUS FTA by making them eligible for subsidies of up to 75 % of their payroll for one year if they switched to another industry or relocated their employees. The government also pledged to provide cash incentives of up to $600 a month to companies that hired farmers and fishermen who had been dislocated from their work (Chosun Ilbo 2007).

In April 2008, President Lee's government announced it would lift the ban on the importation of American beef, supposedly the final barrier to the ratification of the KORUS FTA. Imports of American beef had been virtually halted since 2003 after the detection of mad cow disease in the US. The administration of George W. Bush claimed it had resolved the mad cow problem and that US beef was safe for consumption. Key US lawmakers signaled that ratification of the KORUS FTA hinged on the lifting of the Korean ban. The announcement that US beef imports would resume, with some restrictions on the types of meat to be allowed, sparked a series of mass demonstrations across Korea. This seriously damaged the legitimacy of the new Lee administration (Hundt 2008, pp. 508–509).

As large-scale candlelight demonstrations and protests, along with anti-FTA sentiments, flared up in June 2008, the government had to postpone its announcement on the safety of US beef imports. President Lee also reversed his previous stance against renegotiations, announcing that "if it is the wish of the people, then we will not import beef from cattle over 30 months old." On June 21, the Korean and US governments confirmed a voluntary private sector arrangement that excluded import of beef from cattle over the age of 30 months, as well as beef products from the brain, eyes, spinal cord, and cranial bones of cattle (Jurenas and Manyin 2010, p. 8).

In 2010, during the additional negotiations held in Columbia (Maryland) from November 30 to December 3, Korea made additional concessions to the US in the automobile sector, while gaining American concessions in the areas of beef, pork, pharmaceuticals, and visas. On December 3, the Korean and US governments reached an agreement to modify the KORUS FTA by resolving bilateral differences over beef and automobile issues. The following year, on October 12, the US Congress passed the KORUS FTA, which was the largest free trade deal for the US since the North American Free Trade Agreement. About a month after the congressional move, the National Assembly of Korea also ratified the bilateral trade deal, finally ending a 4.5-year long legislative battle on both sides of the Pacific. The long overdue, but triumphant, story of the KORUS FTA shows that the Lee administration remained committed to the multitrack FTA strategy originally designed by the administration of President Roh. As summarized in Table 6.3, the conclusion of FTA deals with major economies like India and the EU during Lee's presidency also proves the point.[23]

The continuity of the FTA strategy can be traced to the Lee administration's grand foreign policy goals. With the slogan "Global Korea," President Lee urged his people to practice not just passive liberalization but ever more proactive globalization. He increased Korea's foreign assistance, encouraged internationalization among its people, demanded that Seoul become an international hub, and sought a more active participatory role in global governance mechanisms such as the G-20. Since his electoral victory in December 2007, Lee promoted global

---

[23] At the ceremony concluding the Korea-EU FTA negotiations on July 13, 2009, President Lee expressed his hope and belief that Korea's lagging service industry would benefit from freer trade with the EU as a powerhouse of the global service industry, accounting for 46.5 % of global trade in services (Chosun Ilbo 2009).

Table 6.3   Korea's multitrack FTA negotiations

Signed[a]	Under negotiation[b]	Joint study
Chile (0.8 %, 2003, 2004)	Japan (10.3 %, 2003)	Korea-China-Japan (34.4 %)
Singapore (2.6 %, 2005, 2006)	Canada (0.9 %, 2005)	South Africa (0.4 %)
European Free Trade Association (1.0 %, 2005, 2006)	Mexico (1.2 %, 2006)	Russia (2.0 %)
Association of Southeast Asian Nations (ASEAN)[c] (10.9 %, 2006, 2007)	Gulf Cooperation Council (8.8 %, 2008)	Israel (0.2 %)
United States (10.1 %, 2007, 2011)	Australia (3.0 %, 2009)	Vietnam (1.4 %)
India (1.9 %, 2009, 2010)	New Zealand (0.2 %, 2009)	Mercosur (1.7 %)
Peru (0.2 %, 2010, 2011)	China[d] (24.1 %, 2012)	
European Union (10.3 %, 2010, 2011)		
Colombia (0.2 %, 2012, N/A)		
Turkey (0.5 %, 2012, N/A)		

Percentage scores indicate the value of bilateral trade as a portion of Korea's total trade (exports plus imports) in 2010

Sources International Monetary Fund; World Bank

[a]The figures after the percentage scores indicate the year of signing the agreement and the year of the agreement coming into force (updated as of August 2012)

[b]The figures after the % scores indicate the year of the launch of official negotiations

[c]The Korea-ASEAN framework agreement on comprehensive economic cooperation was signed in December 2005; the Korea-ASEAN agreement on trade in goods was signed in August 2006 and came into force in June 2007; the Korea-ASEAN agreement on trade in services was signed in November 2007 and came into force in May 2009; the Korea-ASEAN agreement on investment was signed in June (Dieter 2009) and came into force in September 2009

[d]Including Hong Kong

projects and emphasized inward foreign investment. Indeed, Global Korea had become a centerpiece of Lee's foreign policy initiative, both domestically and internationally (Lee and Hewison 2010).

To summarize, Korea's multitrack FTA initiative has adopted developmental liberalism; greater trade openness in favor of internationally competitive sectors and generous side payments for those who might be hurt by trade liberalization. Most notably, the Roh and Lee governments envisaged the KORUS FTA as a means for Korean firms to benefit from the economies of scale which access to the US market would allow, and so upgrade their competitive edge. In what has been dubbed a version of new industrial policy, Korean firms could thus compete with their Chinese and Japanese counterparts (Woo 2007, pp. 126–127). This policy shift nicely captures a different kind of dualism—that is, proactivism when selecting FTA partners and embeddedness when garnering domestic political support. On the one hand, the OMT institutionalized the idea of pursuing economic reforms and cementing strategic partnerships through FTAs. On the other hand, the success of its proactive negotiations has been achieved by social embeddedness consisting of generous compensation packages to support those who had been disadvantaged by the FTAs. Even with these changes, the most important feature of Korea's new trade strategy is that the reform process continues to reflect the legacies of the developmental state, with the state still playing an important role in planning, implementing, and sustaining economic reform.

6.4 Conclusion and Policy Implications

Korea's mercantilist trade policy traces back to its developmental period that started in the early 1960s and led to the successful story of export-oriented industrialization, often dubbed the "miracle on the Han River" in the 1970s. This chapter argues that it was a good example of developmental mercantilism. However, the political and economic conditions, both external and internal, that underpinned Korea's traditional trade policy paradigm came under heavy pressure at the end of the 1990s. Among other things, the outbreak of the Asian financial crisis of 1997–1998 was a painful wake-up call to seriously consider remodeling Korea's mercantilist policy bias. Its departure from a traditional, top-down trade policy centered on export promotion and import protection can be best illustrated by its active pursuit of FTAs. Korea has led the race toward FTAs in East Asia since it concluded the first cross-Pacific free trade deal with Chile in 2002. This trend took its most pronounced turn when the country concluded an FTA with the world's largest economy, the US, in 2007. The global economic crisis of 2008–2009 has not reduced the speed or scope of Korea's FTA initiative, as demonstrated by the conclusion of trade agreements with India in 2009 and the EU in 2010. The tale of Korea is particularly intriguing because the country has not only been one of the principal beneficiaries of postwar multilateral trading regimes, but has also been criticized for its allegedly protectionist policies.

From an analytical point of view, the significance of Korea's FTA initiative is three-fold. First, it constitutes a notable policy shift toward liberalism, departing from a mercantilist approach characterized by a policy mix of import protection and export promotion. Second, it has been shaped by a top-down political initiative rather than a bottom-up demand from business groups and the general public. Korea's dramatic embrace of FTA policy thus contains a developmental state characteristic. But it also incorporates liberal elements.

The economic crisis of 1997–1998 contributed to the rise of the reform-minded Kim Dae-jung. In pursuit of his diplomatic and economic vision, President Kim was drawn to bilateral and minilateral FTAs, shifting Korea's trade policy focus from global multilateralism to regional/cross-regional bilateralism and minilateralism. And finally, despite Korea's liberal but state-centric nature, its unique partisan politics has led its FTAs to be closely embedded in the country's social fabric, both competitive and uncompetitive. President Kim's grand regionalist vision and liberal economic reforms inspired President Roh Moo-hyun. Yet, in the face of Korea's vocal protectionist interests, the Roh government chose to provide generous side payments to pacify them. As a result, the country's FTA initiative combines developmental embeddedness and liberalism—with this paradigm shift being a key feature of the Lee administration.

This chapter shows that developmental liberalism is increasingly becoming a prominent attribute of Korea's trade policy. Although it is not clear whether and to what extent the trajectory of this trade policy can be replicated in developing countries, one clear lesson can be drawn from Korea's EOI, as backed by neomercantilism: it was made successful only under an unusual combination of international and domestic circumstances, including the Korean War, Japanese colonialism, US hegemony during the Cold War, President Park's strong leadership supported by a capable and committed bureaucracy, and a strong sense of nationalism. It is equally important to note that Korea's embrace of liberal trade policy in the aftermath of the Asian financial crisis does not indicate that it has completely abandoned its top-down approach to trade liberalization. The developmental state model, and its embedded mercantilist variant, may not be valid and will not serve well in the future. However, the Korean government's social embeddedness persists in its top-down pursuit of FTAs. To conclude, the right balance between embeddedness and laissez-faire policy may continue to evolve across time and space.

References

Amsden, A. H. (1989). *Asia's next giant: Korea and late industrialization*. New York, NY: Oxford University Press.

Bergsten, F. (2000, July 13). Towards a tripartite world, *The Economist*, pp. 20–22.

Bridges, B. (1993). *Japan and Korea in the 1990s: From antagonism to adjustment*. Bookfield, VT: Edward Elgar Publishing.

Cha, V. D. (1996). Bridging the gap: The strategic context of the 1965 Korea-Japan normalization treaty. *Korean Studies, 20*, 123–160.

Chang, K.-S. (2007). The end of developmental citizenship? Restructuring and social displacement in post-crisis Korea. *Economic and Political Weekly, 42*(50), 67–72.

Cheong, I. (1999). *Economic impact of a Korea-Chile FTA and Its implications to Korean economy*. KIEP (in Korean): Seoul.

Chosun Ilbo (2006a, January 26). *Screen quota cut clears way for Trade deal with US*. http://english.chosun.com/site/data/html_dir/2006/01/26/2006012661013.html.

Chosun Ilbo (2006b, January 27).*Will the post-screen quota measures be effective?* http://news.chosun.com/site/data/html_dir/2006/01/27/2006012770343.html.

Chosun Ilbo (2007, June 29). *Government to pay farmers, fishermen for FTA losses*. http://english.chosun.com/site/data/html_dir/2007/06/29/2007062961022.html.

Chosun Ilbo (2009, July 14). FTA a chance to Bolster Korea's lagging service Industry. http://english.chosun.com/site/data/html_dir/2009/07/14/2009071400678.html.

Dieter, H. (2009). Changing patterns of regional governance: From security to political economy? *The Pacific Review, 22*(1), 73–90.

Hundt, D. (2008). Korea: Squandering a mandate for change? *Australian Journal of International Affairs, 62*(4), 497–512.

International Monetary Fund, *Direction of Trade Statistics Yearbook (CD-ROM)*. Washington, D.C.: International Monetary Fund.

Jurenas, R. & Mark E. M. (2010, September 23). *US-Korea beef dispute: Issues and status*. Washington, DC: Congressional Research Service RL34528, Report for Members and Committees of Congress. http://assets.opencrs.com/rpts/RL34528_20100923.pdf.

Kim, S. (2011). Globalization and national responses: The case of Korea. *International Review of Public Administration, 16*(2), 165–179.

Koo, M. G. (2006) From multilateralism to bilateralism? A shift in Korea's trade strategy. In V. K. Aggarwal & S. Urata (Eds.), *Bilateral trade agreements in the Asia-Pacific: origins, evolution, and implications.* New York, NY: Routledge, pp. 140–59.

Koo, M. G. (2009a). *Island disputes and maritime regime building in East Asia: between a rock and a hard place.* New York, NY: Springer.

Koo, M. G. (2009b). Korea's FTAs: Moving from an emulative to a competitive strategy. In M. Solis, B. Stallings, & S. N. Katada (Eds.), *Competitive regionalism: FTA diffusion in the pacific rim* (pp. 181–197). Palgrave Macmillan: New York, NY.

Koo, M. G. (2010). Embracing free trade agreements Korean style: From developmental mercantilism to developmental liberalism. *The Korean Journal of Policy Studies, 25*(3), 101–123.

Kwon, H. (2005). Transforming the developmental welfare state in East Asia. *Development and Change, 36*(3), 477–497.

Lee, J.-H. (1990). Korean-Japanese relations: The past present and future. *Korea Observer, 21*(2), 159–178.

Lee, D. (1995a). *A true record of Park Chung-Hee and Korea-Japan treaty negotiations: from 5–16 to its conclusion (in Korean).* Seoul: Hansong.

Lee, W. D. (1995b). The process of the Korea-Japan treaty. In The institute of national issues (Ed.), *The Korea-Japan treaty revisited* (In Korean). Seoul: Asia Publications.

Lee, S. (2006, April) *The political economy of the Korea-US FTA: The Korean government's FTA strategy revisited* (in Korean). Paper presented at the convention of the Association of Korean Political and Diplomatic History.

Lee, S. –J., Han, T. (2006). The demise of "Korea, Inc.": Paradigm shift in Korea's developmental state, *Journal of Contemporary Asia, 36*(3), pp. 305–24.

Lee, S.-J., & Hewison, K. (2010). Introduction: Korea and the antinomies of neo-liberal globalization. *Journal of Contemporary Asia, 40*(2), 181–187.

Lim, H. (2010). The transformation of the developmental state and economic reform in Korea. *Journal of Contemporary Asia, 40*(2), 188–210.

Ministry of Finance and Economy (2005, November 22). *Economic Bulletin, 27*(11), Seoul: Ministry of Finance and Economy.

Ministry of Foreign Affairs and Trade. (2004). *Rules regarding the special law to support farmers and fishermen as a result of FTAs.* Seoul: Ministry of Foreign Affairs and Trade. http://www.fta.go.kr/pds/data/200407224131655자유무역협정체결에따른농어업인등의 지원에관한특별법시행규칙.pdf

Ministry of Foreign Affairs and Trade. (2006). *Key initiatives of year 2006.* Seoul: Ministry of Foreign Affairs and Trade.

National Emergency Conference. (2007, March). *Appeal to the Korean people.* Seoul: National Emergency Conference to Urge to Stop the Rushed Korea-US FTA Negotiation. http://www.demos.or.kr/bbs/view.php?id=english&page=1&sn1=&divpage=1&sn=off&ss=on&sc=on&select_arrange=headnum&desc=asc&no=74

Office of the United States Trade Representative. (2006). *The 2006 national trade estimate report on foreign trade barriers.* Washington, DC: Office of the United States Trade Representative.

Pempel, T. J. (1998). *Regime shift: Comparative dynamics of the Japanese political economy.* Ithaca, NY: Cornell University Press.

Pempel, T. J. (1999). Regional ups, regional downs. In T. J. Pempel (Ed.), *The politics of the Asian economic crisis* (pp. 62–78). Ithaca, NY: Cornell University Press.

Sohn, C.–H. (2001, June 12–13). *Korea's FTA developments: Experiences and perspectives with Chile, Japan, and the US.* Paper presented at a conference of the Pacific Economic Cooperation Council Trade Policy Forum on Regional Trading Arrangements: Stocktake and Next Steps, Bangkok.

Sohn, Y., & Koo, M. G. (2011). Securitizing trade: The case of the Korea-US free trade agreement. *International Relations of the Asia-Pacific, 11*(3), 433–460.

Wade, R. (2000). Wheels within wheels: Rethinking the Asian crisis and the Asian model. *Annual Review of Political Science, 3*, 85–115.

Woo, M. J. (2007). East Asia after the financial crisis. In The Korea Herald (ed.), *Insight into Korea: Understanding challenges of the 21st century*. Seoul: Herald Media.

Woo-Cumings, M. (1999). Introduction: Chalmers Johnson and the politics of nationalism and development. In M. Woo Cumings (Ed.), *The developmental state*. Ithaca: Cornell University Press.

World Bank, *World Development Indicators*, Washington, D.C.: The World Bank. http://data.worldbank.org/data-catalog/world-development-indicators.

Yamazawa, I. (1990). *Economic development and international trade: The Japanese model*. Honolulu, HI: University of Hawaii Press.

Chapter 7
Educational Policy, Development of Education, and Economic Growth in Korea

Shin-Bok Kim

7.1 Introduction

It is a well-known fact that national development in Korea—especially the rapid economic growth—has taken place largely because of the country's highly educated, but low-paid, human resources. The scope and objectives of this chapter aim to describe changes in major educational policies in the 60 years since the establishment of the government in 1948; review the quantitative and qualitative development of education; and explore the contribution of educational development to economic progress. The first part of this chapter will overview changes and reforms in educational policies during the past six decades. Next, it will examine the characteristics of Korean education quantitatively and qualitatively. Finally, it will introduce major studies on the contribution of education to productivity and economic growth in Korea.

7.2 Changes in the Educational System and Policy

7.2.1 The Role of Government in Education

Korean education features a centralized education governance system. The importance of the government's role in education has always been well-recognized. It can clearly be seen in article 31 of the country's constitution, which stipulates the responsibilities of the government regarding education:

S.-B. Kim (✉)
Graduate School of Public Administration, Seoul National University, Seoul 151-742,
Republic of Korea
e-mail: sbkim1@snu.ac.kr

H. Kwon and M. G. Koo (eds.), *The Korean Government and Public Policies in a Development Nexus, Volume 1*, The Political Economy of the Asia Pacific, DOI: 10.1007/978-3-319-01098-4_7, © Springer International Publishing Switzerland 2014

- compulsory education shall be free of charge;
- the state shall promote lifelong education; and
- fundamental matters pertaining to the educational system shall be determined by act.

The government has the authority to make decisions about key issues in education, such as staffing, budget, and curriculum. Korea has had a national curriculum since 1949, and the education minister has the exclusive authority to approve textbooks for primary and secondary schools.

The government, by law, also regulates qualifications, promotions, in-service training, and deployment of teachers in public or private schools. In addition, public school teachers are transferred periodically, once every 4 or 5 years, to decrease the gaps in educational conditions among schools.

Private schools in Korea do not have much autonomy, even though they are not public schools. They can hire teachers as they wish, except that the teachers are required to have a national teaching certificate. Private schools also have to comply—like public schools—with the regulatory framework of the national curriculum and textbooks. While the government requires private schools to charge the same amount of tuition as public ones, private schools have structural deficits which the government is to subsidize by comparing the tuition with the national standard cost of education. In keeping with the high school equalization policy (HSEP), adopted in 1974, most private high schools in city areas do not have the right to select their students, and regional education authorities, therefore, assign students to both private and public schools in much the same way.

7.2.2 Policy Changes in Education

Following the establishment of the Republic of Korea in 1948, an education law was enacted on the basis of democratic principles. The government adopted a 6-3-3-4 school system and declared that 6 years of education at the primary level would be compulsory. In order to eliminate illiteracy, the government also introduced extensive adult education, as well as supplementary in-service training for teachers.

In the midst of the Korean War (1950–1953), efforts were continued to revive education to fulfill the goal of overcoming the national crisis and spearheading reconstruction. Remarkable economic progress—and subsequent drastic changes in politics, society, and culture—brought about a quantitative expansion, which is a feature of Korean education in the 1960s and 1970s. This expansion included an explosive increase in the number of students, teachers, and educational facilities. A rapid growth in the school-age population resulted inevitably in overcrowded classrooms, oversized schools, a shortage of qualified teachers, and educational facilities, with excessive competition in college entrance examinations (Ministry of Education/MOE 2000). Accordingly, reform measures were instituted to restore school education to its normal state. Major policies were employed to:

- reform teacher training;
- upgrade primary school teachers from normal high schools to junior colleges, and standardize the 4-year college education for secondary school teachers;
- abolish entrance examinations to middle school (1968);
- implement the HSEP; and
- carry out preliminary tests for college admission.

In the 1980s, Korea endeavored to control and enhance the quality of its education. The administration of President Chun Doo-hwan clearly established the institutionalization of lifelong education in the country's constitution. In addition, the government set as its top priority the formation of sound character through education, as well as the reform of general education, emphasizing science and lifelong learning. Some of the actions taken during this period helped to:

- launch exclusive education programs through the Educational Broadcasting System (EBS);
- introduce the July 30 Education Reform (1980), with a graduation quota system for colleges and universities;
- initiate an education tax to secure financial resources for educational investment;
- abolish entrance examinations administered by individual colleges, requiring universities to reflect high school achievement in entrance examinations; and
- promulgate the Non-formal Education Act and Kindergarten Education Support Act.

The Korean government has emphasized human education since 1990, which was pursuing to cultivate future citizenship on the basis of upgrading the quality of education in the 1980s. Particular concerns were the pursuit of qualitative development—rather than quantitative growth—and the fulfillment of high public demand for education by extending compulsory education, popularizing secondary education and increasing opportunities for higher education. The ultimate goal of schooling in this period was to contribute to personal self-realization and national development. Consequently, the direction of educational policies was established: attainment of sound character, quest for excellence, realization of equality, and enhancement of hope for a better future (MOE 2000).

In 1995, the government began comprehensive education reform to eradicate chronic educational problems. The underlying principle of the reform was to enable all students to cultivate their capabilities and creativity, and improve the flexibility of the education system. In this way, they could enjoy learning through their own interests at any time and in any place. The school was regarded as the unit of change, and the focus was on changing the culture that existed within primary and secondary schools.

In 1999, the Ministry of Education (MOE) launched a reform project for higher education, known as Brain Korea 21 (BK21). The government invested a total of $1.2 billion over 7 years to develop world-class graduate schools and local universities, enhancing the graduate schools' research capabilities and building infrastructure for academic research. The government also started a project in 1999 to nurture regional universities that would meet the demand and needs of local industry, with $285 million invested over a 7-year period (MOE 2000). Education reform was systematically implemented by the government to:

- establish strategic planning for human resources development;
- consolidate primary and secondary schooling to strengthen the nation's basic education;
- enhance the quality of college education to bring it to the level of economically advanced nations;
- encourage lifelong learning and vocational training to develop an ability-oriented society;
- invigorate the teaching profession;
- pursue informationization and globalization of Korean education; and
- set up an educational administration and financial structure for successful education reform.

7.3 Quantitative Expansion of Education

7.3.1 Educational Opportunity

Korea is one of the few developing countries that has implemented a policy of automatic grade promotion at all levels. Enrollment in primary schools is almost equally distributed across the six grades, and most children are the right age for their grade.

Beginning in 1968, entrance examinations to middle school for pupils from the primary level were eliminated. In effect, students were automatically promoted from the sixth to the seventh grade. Not all applied for entrance to middle school, however, perhaps because of higher fees or greater opportunity costs. But the proportion of students going to middle school was much higher than that found in most developing countries, and was equivalent to transition rates in the more economically advanced countries. Between 1964 and 1971, a total of 75.6 % of males and 55.8 % of females went on to middle school (Kim 1973a, b). By 1974, the figures had risen to 83.0 % and 67.1 %, respectively. These rates are practically

Table 7.1 School enrollment rate: student/school-age population (in percent)

	Primary school	Middle school	High school	Tertiary education
1951	69.8	n.a.	n.a.	n.a.
1959	96.4	n.a.	n.a.	n.a.
1970	92.0	36.6	20.3	5.4
1980	97.7	73.3	48.8	11.4
1990	100.5	91.6	79.4	23.6
2000	97.2	95.0	89.4	52.5
2010	98.6	97.6	92.4	70.1

Source Korean Educational Development Institute (2010)

Table 7.2 Advancement rate (in percent)

	Primary school → middle school	Middle school → high school	High school → tertiary education
1970	66.1	70.1	26.9
1980	95.8	84.5	27.2
1990	99.8	95.7	33.2
2000	99.9	99.6	68.0
2010	99.9	99.7	79.0

Source KEDI (2010)

equivalent to automatic promotion, and are consistent with the announced intention of the government to make middle school education compulsory by 1981. Since the 1990s, almost all applicants could enter both middle and high school. The rate of advancement to higher education grew rapidly, especially since the 1990s, and is now among the highest in the world (Tables 7.1 and 7.2).

7.3.2 Facilities and Teachers

The public cost of education has been lower in Korea than in other comparable countries. In 1970, public expenditure per student at all three levels of education was estimated to be as follows: primary school, $40; middle school, $77; and high school $97. Low costs were realized in two major ways. First, teachers received relatively moderate salaries. Second, class size was very large, thus distributing the cost of instruction over a larger number of students (McGinn et al. 1980).

Class sizes were particularly large after the Korean War, as might be expected. There has been a steady increase in class size in all except primary school, in which enrollment peaked in 1970. An average class of 50–60 included a number of much larger classes. For example, in 1965, 11 % of primary school classrooms held more than 90 students, and another 26 % between 81 and 90 students (McGinn et al. 1980). Though class size and students per teacher have gradually decreased in primary and secondary schools, they have grown remarkably in colleges and universities. The main reason for pupil/teacher ratios in colleges being much higher than those in primary and secondary schools was the shortage of public investment in tertiary education (Tables 7.3 and 7.4).

7.3.3 Financial Support

The great expansion of education since 1945 could not have been realized if the state had assumed the entire burden of financing it. A number of developing countries today find themselves at an impasse, being unable to enlarge primary educational opportunity to attain universal enrollment because of its expense, which seriously strains the national budget (Kim 1973a, b).

Table 7.3 Trends in class size (number of students)

	Primary school	Middle school	General high school	Vocational high school
1970	62.5	62.1	60.1	56.1
1980	51.5	62.1	59.9	59.6
1990	41.4	50.2	53.6	51.5
2000	35.8	38.0	44.1	40.3
2010	26.6	33.8	35.5	29.1

Source KEDI (2010)

Table 7.4 Trends in students per teacher

	Primary school	Middle school	General high school	Vocational high school	Junior college	University
1970	56.9	42.3	32.0	27.5	24.2	22.4
1980	47.5	45.1	33.9	32.6	33.8	34.2
1990	35.6	25.4	25.4	23.4	52.7	41.1
2000	28.7	20.1	20.9	18.2	78.0	39.7
2010	18.7	18.2	16.5	13.1	61.2	36.2

Source KEDI (2010)

Table 7.5 Share of students in private schools (in percent)

	Primary school	Middle school	General high school	Vocational high school	Junior college	University
1970	1.1	48.6	60.4	48.1	57.0	75.4
1980	1.3	38.8	61.8	56.5	83.7	71.5
1990	1.4	28.6	61.7	61.7	91.7	75.5
2000	1.3	22.1	57.1	50.9	95.9	77.7

Source KEDI (2010)

An explanation for the low public cost of education in Korea is that parents are expected to contribute to the support of schools and teachers, which is over and above their contributions through taxes. Until the 1990s, the Korean government provided fewer subsidies for secondary and higher education than other developing countries. Figures in Table 7.5 reflect the large private contributions to higher levels of education.

In addition to the cost of books and meals, parents have also had to pay for uniforms, transportation, school equipment, and other expenses. The parents' payment of these costs relieved the government of a considerable recurrent burden. The private share of enrollment in middle and high schools rose from 31 and 26 %, respectively in 1953 to 1949 and 55 % in 1970. These increases indicate the extent to which the government had "saved" on education (McGinn et al. 1980). The share of private institutions has been very high in tertiary education, mainly because the government allowed the establishment of private universities to supplement scarce public funds.

As the Korean economy grew rapidly after the 1960s, and the number of students increased, expenditure on education expanded remarkably not only in its

Table 7.6 Educational expenditure by funding source, as ratio of GDP (in percent)

	Funding source	Korea					OECD average	United States	Japan
		1977	1985	1990	2000	2001	2001	2001	2001
Total		4.60	5.73	4.86	7.10	8.20	5.70	7.40	4.70
	Public	2.44	3.13	2.97	4.30	4.80	5.00	5.10	3.50
	Private	2.16	2.60	1.89	2.80	3.40	0.70	2.30	1.20
Pre-primary		–	0.07	0.09	0.50	0.10	0.40	0.50	0.20
	Public	–	0.02	0.02	n.a.	n.a.	n.a.	n.a.	n.a.
	Private	–	0.05	0.07	n.a.	n.a.	n.a.	n.a.	n.a.
Primary and		3.82	3.98	3.44	4.00	4.60	3.80	4.10	2.90
secondary	Public	2.22	2.59	2.47	3.30	n.a.	n.a.	n.a.	n.a.
	Private	1.60	1.39	0.97	0.70	n.a.	n.a.	n.a.	n.a.
Tertiary		0.78	1.68	1.33	2.50	2.70	1.30	2.70	1.10
	Public	0.22	0.52	0.48	0.60	0.40	1.00	0.90	0.50
	Private	0.56	1.16	0.85	1.90	2.30	0.30	1.80	0.60

Source Lee (2005)

aggregate amount but also in relative ratio to gross domestic product (GDP). The share of total educational expenditure relative to GDP increased from 4.6 % in 1977 to 8.2 % in 2001. Classifying educational expenditure by funding sources, public financing increased to 4.8 % in 2001, which is slightly lower than the average percentage for countries of the Organization for Economic Co-operation and Development (OECD). In contrast, the ratio of private burden to GDP has been much higher than the OECD average, with the result that Korea expended the highest percentage of educational funds relative to GDP among OECD countries.

The government expanded public financing of education and placed a high priority on budget allocation. Private burden also climbed during the same period, especially for tertiary education. It is noteworthy that the ratio of public financing of higher education to GDP is relatively small compared to other countries of the OECD (Table 7.6).

7.3.4 Government Strategies

The sustained expansion of educational opportunities brought about universal school enrollment in Korea. Accepting the criteria of universal access to education as the achievement of 90 % enrollment, or a 90 % entrance rate to the next school level, primary school education was universalized in 1957, middle school education in 1979, and high school education in 1985. Since 1995, the entrance rate from high school to tertiary institutions began to exceed 50 %. The average number of years spent in the education system rose from five in 1965 to 10.6 in 2001 (Song 2003). This quantitative expansion of Korean education was helped by some government strategies that sought to:

- achieve universal access to primary school education at an early stage of educational expansion;
- employ a sequential, bottom-up approach to widen opportunities for primary education, followed by middle school and high school education;
- apply a low-cost approach to encourage access to education at the expense of the quality of classroom conditions;
- use private schools to extend access to secondary education to achieve targeted enrollment;
- procure legal provision to secure funding for education. The Law on Government Grants for Local Education Financing helped facilitate educational access as well as it set aside 12.98 % of total domestic tax revenue for elementary and secondary education; and
- commit to an egalitarian approach to expand access to education. This approach was encouraged by legislative action, such as the abolition of entrance examinations to middle school, and the adoption of the HSEP (Lee et al. 2010).

7.3.5 Unique Attributes

Korean education has grown rapidly, in terms of school enrollment, facilities, and teachers. This growth has occurred at all levels, including in primary and middle schools, academic and vocational secondary schools, as well as in higher education. The rate of growth was as high as—or higher than—that in most countries at all levels of schooling.

A number of unique attributes of education in Korea may have contributed to the system's capacity for rapid expansion after 1945, despite the low levels of national income. They all turn on a very high social demand for education, best explained by the centuries-old tradition of respect for the educated man, combined with a recognition that social and economic positions in modern Korea were closely linked to levels of educational attainment.

One can ask why social demand has been so strong in the Korean case. Part of the answer is no doubt cultural—that is, the recognized importance of study and respect for the scholar in the Confucian tradition. Moreover, the country's traditional system of social class was all but destroyed in the upheavals created by foreign military occupation, the Korean War, and the national partition of the South and North. These histories might well have weakened many of the influences that would strongly condition social mobility in other countries, leaving education as a uniquely important means of personal advancement. This would also explain the fierce competition for places at the higher levels of the school system, which may do little to actually make people more productive, but play an important role in their success in gaining access to high income jobs and enviable social positions (McGinn et al. 1980).

Associated with this importance of education is the privileged social position of the teacher, a cultural heritage from the Chinese, reinforced under the Japanese. In Korea, the teacher's social status has been high, and it has been possible to attract large numbers of educated people to teach even in primary schools (Kim 1996). Similar situations can be found in relatively few other countries.

This attribute goes hand-in-hand with the ability of Korean teachers to command absolute respect from their students. While teachers in many other parts of the world may spend much of their class hours on problems of discipline rather than instruction, the Korean teacher can expect that students will discipline themselves.

Some of the unique features of education in Korea should, in terms of conventional wisdom, contribute to insufficient educational conditions. For example, class size in Korean schools is very large, and on an average, teachers face about twice as many students as the standard which educational specialists claim is desirable. Classes are large not only in primary schools but also in secondary and technical/vocational schools. Second, although many educators favor automatic grade promotion as a device to reduce inequality—introduced by "streaming" and "screening" in education—it runs counter to recommendations for "ability grouping" and "special training" for the more talented students. Automatic grade promotion has now been applied in Korea at all levels of the system. Third, educational specialists argue that the most effective education is to teach students how to think, rather than what to think. The emphasis on rote memorization, learning of facts rather than principles, encyclopedic curricula—all of these are seen as counterproductive, and are often cited as typical of education in backward areas (McGinn et al. 1980). These criticisms have been made against school education in Korea.

However, there are other features of Korean education that would be looked upon positively by most education specialists. The most striking feature is the extent of private spending on schooling. Korean families have had to carry most of the financial load, paying fees even in public schools and relying heavily on private schooling when the government was slow to expand public school capacity. It is the willingness of large numbers of Korean families to pay these substantial amounts, which are large, especially relative to their modest incomes.

7.4 Qualitative Development of Education

7.4.1 Content and Quality of Teaching Until the 1980s

The most distinctive content and method of instruction in Korean schools, from that found in many other developing countries, may be that the curriculum tends to reinforce social integration rather than weaken it, as all students are treated equally. While students are in school, they enjoy or suffer the same destiny. Less clear is to what extent students in Korea learned the contents that were considered important for economic development. It has been recognized as a label of Korean education that a curriculum based on the lecture method of instruction and rote memorization by students, combined with preparation for an eventual examination, enhances the legitimacy of the teacher, and facilitates the handling of large classes. Classes of 50–60 students would be impossible in primary schools if teachers were obliged to work with each student individually, or if students were encouraged to pursue their own interests and to challenge the teacher as the sole source of knowledge (McGinn et al. 1980).

Although objectives were set for the introduction of a vocational/techni-cal emphasis in schools, not much progress had been made toward these objec-tives until the country's economic takeoff. The emphasis on individualism and productivity in the curriculum of the 1950s was replaced by greater emphasis on collectivity and conformity in the 1960s. There were—and apparently still are—considerable disparities between objectives held by the national executive and those held by administrators and teachers (and parents) at the local level, where education takes place. What distinguished the curriculum in Korean schools from that of countries whose attempts at development had failed was not its emphasis on science and technology until the 1970s. With a growing demand for skilled workers since the 1970s, however, the government began to lay stress on voca-tional education, followed by financial support to modernize school equipment and facilities by means of the national budget or overseas loans (McGinn et al. 1980).

Korea made significant investment in the 1960s in family planning education. The effects of that campaign, in terms of reduced birth rates and declining population growth rates, began to appear after the economy took off. Also, the New Community Movement—*Saemaul Undong*—made a notable contribution to the use of nonformal education in an integrated campaign for total community development in the 1970s.

In sum, the expansion of education in Korea could occur at the lower levels of per capita income because the quality of education was commensurate with the eco-nomic levels of society. That is, in contrast with many other countries, Korea chose a policy of adaptation, rather than providing sufficient conditions during the decades from the 1950s to the 1980s. Korean education has not improved according to con-ventional indicators of educational quality, although the general quality is doubtlessly high. Class sizes have been relatively big and unit costs have not grown, if they are compared to the national economy and income levels of the people until the 1990s.

7.4.2 Government Efforts to Improve Quality of Education

During the 1980s–1990s, the Korean government expanded its investment in edu-cation and established various administrative reforms and regulations in order to improve the quality of education. As shown earlier (Sects. 7.3.3 and 7.3.4), an increase in the education budget has brought about a striking improvement in school conditions, including facilities and teaching staff. As part of its institutional reform policy, the government upgraded junior colleges of education to 4-year col-leges to train primary school teachers, and augmented teachers' salaries, making the teaching profession more attractive. The colleges of education responsible for instructing secondary school teachers have produced three times as many gradu-ates with teaching certificates than the number of teaching jobs available. As a result, there has been intense competition for recruitment as teachers.

Since the latter half of the 1990s, information and communications technology has been widely used in school management and the development of instructional programs. The government launched a website, known as EDUNET, to deliver educational materials to the classroom and to provide educational information network services that are a major source of academic information for research purposes.

The EBS was established in the 1980s to broadcast educational programs that linked directly to classrooms in primary and secondary schools. As private tutoring was seen as a serious social problem, the EBS began to impart low-cost supplementary tutoring programs on television as an alternative to private coaching.

Korean education has witnessed the determining impact of college entrance examinations on the content and mode of teaching and learning in public education. The competitiveness of the entrance examinations has encouraged private tutoring. As the assessment of student achievement scores in high schools provides universities with data for selecting applicants, the government appealed to all universities to give greater weight to these scores, and to the performance of students in a variety of fields, rather than rely simply on the results of written college entrance tests (Lee et al. 2010).

Besides the internal assessment conducted by schools, external institutes are also used to conduct assessments of student achievement. Teachers' organizations are opposed to revealing details of student achievement, especially where there is disparity among classes, schools, or regions. Since the 1990s, various kinds of evaluation models have been applied to education programs. The administrative authorities have evaluated universities, provincial boards of education, and primary and secondary schools.

The first priority of the government in the early 2000s was to reform higher education to enhance its relevance to societal needs and the international competitiveness of the country's universities. BK21 (see Sect. 7.2.2) was a new project to support research-oriented graduate programs in select universities. The New University for Regional Innovation program, meanwhile, was designed to support universities in their effort to develop human resources in regional communities (Ministry of Education and Human Resources Development 2001).

The MOE has promoted specific policy measures to foster lifelong education within the context of the formal education system. Universities have begun to play a more important role in providing lifelong learning programs. The number of primary and secondary schools which participate in extracurricular activities has increased as well. In addition, corporations have been encouraged—and supported—in their provision of educational services through corporate college programs.

7.4.3 Quality and Equity of Student Achievement After the 1990s

The first results of the Program for International Student Assessment (PISA) 2000 were published in 2001, showing how well 15-year-olds in the OECD and other countries could apply their knowledge and skills in key subject areas. The results revealed wide differences, not just among countries, but also among schools and students within countries.

In Finland and Korea, only around 5 % of students performed at the lowest level, and <2 % below it, but these two countries were exceptions. In all of the other countries, 10 % or more of students performed at, or below, the lowest level. However, the overall results of PISA 2000 were encouraging. The performance of countries, such as Finland and Korea, showed that excellence in schooling is attainable at reasonable cost. For example, Ireland and Korea were among the best performing countries, but spent <\$35,000 per student up to the age of 15 years, well below the OECD average of \$45,000 (OECD 2002).

Korea, Canada, Finland, Iceland, Japan, and Sweden displayed above-average levels of student performance in reading literacy and, at the same time, demonstrated a below-average impact of economic, social, and cultural status on the way students performed (OECD 2002).

In Korea, most of the variation was within schools but, more importantly, both within-and between-school variations were only around half of the OECD average. Korea, thus, not only achieved high average proficiency in reading and low overall disparity among students, but did so with relatively little variation in performance among schools. The three best performing countries—Finland, Japan, and Korea—showed a very moderate degree of institutional differentiation, combined with a consistently high level of student performance across schools and among students from different family backgrounds (OECD 2002).

The results achieved by students in Korea, along with Finland, Canada, and Japan, indicate that it is possible to combine high performance standards with an equitable distribution of learning outcomes. Quality and equity do not have to be seen as competing policy objectives.

The results of PISA 2006 also reveal rankings similar to PISA 2003, as shown in Table 7.7. The ranking of the upper 5 % of students has improved, especially in reading, but has dropped considerably in science. A striking outcome for Korea in PISA 2003 was that the country was ranked first in problem solving, despite a style of education that has been criticized for its lecture method of teaching and rote memorization by students.

Table 7.7 Korean student achievement rankings, based on PISA's triennial assessments

Years	Group	Reading	Math	Science	Problem solving
2009	Total	2-4	3-6	4-7	n.a.
	Upper 5 %	6	5	18	n.a.
2006	Total	1	3	10	n.a.
	Upper 5 %	1	1	7	n.a.
2003	Total	2	3	4	1
	Upper 5 %	7	3	2	3
2000	Total	6	2	1	No test
	Upper 5 %	20	5	5	

Source OECD, PISA Reports, (2000, 2003, 2006, 2009)

7.5 Contribution of Education to Productivity and Economic Growth

At the close of World War II, Korea was a poor and backward nation, just emerging from a history of colonial repression. But, despite limited resources, it had built in a relatively short period of time an exceedingly sound educational system, in terms of provision of educational access to children, usually found in countries with much larger resources and higher levels of national income.

Korea's economic growth had been so rapid that in the space of no more than a few years it has moved up from the ranks of the very poor into the range of middle-income countries in terms of income level, industrialization, and urbanization. The country has overcome not merely the results of a colonial legacy, but also the results of a bloody and destructive war in which most of its stock of human and physical resources was lost. Growth of education and expansion of the economy have been possible, despite the heavy burden of military expenditure associated with the Cold War, in the aftermath of the 1950s conflict.

7.5.1 Education, Human Resources Development, and Productivity

Prior to 1960, education expanded much more rapidly than the economy, to the extent that the educated unemployed were regarded as a serious problem. For several years, the number of graduates, especially in certain technical fields, exceeded the manpower requirements of the economy (Kim 1996). The situation has never been fully corrected, and has resulted from heavy expenditure on education. But some claim that it was the pool of available talent that made possible the economic takeoff in Korea. The remarkable and rapid economic growth has been based to a large degree on human capital, and education has assisted in the production of a literate and industrious people (United Nations Educational, Scientific and Cultural Organization 1974). The accumulation of educated manpower helped lay the foundation for rapid economic growth, which occurred after 1962. The export-oriented pattern of economic development during this period increased the demand for skilled laborers, technicians, engineers, managers, and entrepreneurs. Educational expansion, especially at the secondary and higher levels, had made these workers available. Accelerated economic growth effectively absorbed this educated workforce. Effective use of human resources was reflected in a decline in the unemployment rate and rise in value added per worker, at an average rate of 6.0 % per annum during the period 1963–1975.

Enrollment in vocational high schools has risen since 1965, matching the rise in gross national product (GNP). It has been the government's intention since 1965 to emphasize vocational over academic education at the secondary level, striving for a 60–40 (or 70–30) split in enrollment favoring vocational training. In an effort to

Table 7.8 Rates of return measured by different researchers (in percent)

	Base year	Middle school	High school	College or university
Kwang-Suk Kim	1967	12.0	9.0	5.0
Florida State University	1969	20.0	11.0	9.5
Chang-Yong Chung	1971	8.2	14.6	9.4
Jong-Kun Bae	1977	2.8	9.9	13.8
Se-Il Park	1980	2.0	8.1	11.7
Korean Educationa	1982	9.5	12.3	13.0
Development Institutel	1994	–	7.3	7.2

Source Korean Association of Educational Administration (2003)

overcome traditional resistance to vocational studies, the MOE had offered special incentives to students, including attractive and promising programs of scholarships and employment (Paik 1969). After the 1980s, Korea invested large amounts in skill training for workers, through out-of-factory training programs, apprenticeship schemes, or on-the-job training. Training there must have been, as hundreds of thousands of workers left rural areas to enter the nation's industries.

It is assumed that the value added through the process of education is recognized by the market. Therefore, one can look to the economic value of education as evidence of its contribution to productivity. This value is recognized in various ways. Those who are more highly educated are paid more than those who are less educated. People want education because they know that it contributes to their advancement.

In Korea, as elsewhere, there is a positive rate of return to education. However, the rates of return in Korea are lower than the rates of return to physical capital, unlike in other countries (Jeong 1977). Second, until the 1960s, the rate of return to higher education was lower than that to secondary education, but was reversed after the late 1970s. Finally, it was possible for individuals to have high rates of return to their investment in education without any equivalent increase in GNP, as can be seen in a number of countries with very low growth rates and high returns to education. What influences the rates of return for the most part are income differentials among people with varying levels of educational attainment (Table 7.8)?

7.5.2 Contribution of Education to Economic Growth

Although there are not enough data points to be certain, it would appear that the rate of growth of primary enrollment between 1945 and 1950 was greater than at any period after that time. From 1955 until about 1966–1967, enrollment grew at an almost constant rate, and several times faster than the population growth rate. The rate of growth of enrollment in middle school varied until 1964, bearing no apparent relationship to the development of the economy. Between 1964 and 1970–1971, middle school enrollment grew at the same rate as GNP. Again, it seems reasonable to explain this association on the basis of access to school being determined by the success of the economy. Once the government had provided capacity for all children in primary schools, it began to spend more on middle school construction. When the entrance examination to middle school was eliminated in 1968, enrollment grew faster than GNP, perhaps because changes in the occupational structure of the economy had—by this time—made primary school education insufficient for urban or modern sector employment.

Enrollment in academic secondary schools increased at essentially the same rate as GNP between 1955 and 1965, but has slowed since then. The enlargement of college and university enrollment was highly changeable until 1967. There is no obvious relationship between GNP growth and enrollment fluctuation. Enrollment in higher education has been progressing at a quicker rate than GNP, and the quickest rise in enrollment was prior to 1957.

The educational growth rate reached its highest point more than 10 years before economic takeoff, and the delay was longer than would normally have been expected. A more plausible explanation is that social demand for education outstripped economic need in the early 1950s, resulting in a period of unemployment for the educated workforce. Only when the economy began to heat up, and require larger numbers of workers, was it possible to achieve some balance between GNP growth and growth in education.

Several attempts have been made to measure education's contribution to economic growth in Korea. These have provided different estimates of the magnitude of the contribution made by education, but they are consistent with the view that an important—although perhaps declining—proportion of economic growth after 1960 is attributable to the growth in education.

McGinn et al. conducted a comprehensive and systematic analysis of the contribution of education to development, especially to economic growth from 1945 to 1975. During the period from 1960 to 1974, according to the analysis, GNP grew by an average of 9.07 % per annum, while fixed capital, employment, and quality of labor due to education increased by 7.19 %, 3.55 %, and 1.18 %, respectively. The increase in capital is estimated to have contributed 2.88 % points to the GNP growth rate, and the increase in labor 2.13 % points. Of the remaining 4.06 points, a total of 0.71 % points of GNP growth rate were explained by the qualitative improvement of labor through education (McGinn et al. 1980).

Other research has measured the contribution of education to economic growth during the period from 1966 to 1994, as shown in Table 7.9. It concluded that the quantitative contribution of the labor force was low, but its qualitative contribution because of education and training was relatively high, compared to the period from 1966 to 1975 (Choi 1997).

The estimated percentages of the contribution of education to output growth in Korea exceed those evaluated by Denison for the United States and Europe (Denison 1966). But they are lower than the appraisals carried out in the 1960s by previous researchers. Part of the difference can be explained by an extension of the period in which the estimate is based, since the apparent contribution of education has been relatively minor in recent years.

7.6 Summary and Conclusion

Korea has maintained a centralized governance system in educational administration. The government has exercised strong control not only over national and
public schools, but also over private schools. Educational policies and reforms
in Korea have focused on expanding educational conditions and mitigating the
intensely competitive entrance examinations, in response to an abnormally high
demand for education. Typical examples include the 6-3-3-4 unitary school system introduced in 1948; the 6-year compulsory education plan from 1954 to 1959;
abolition of middle school entrance examinations in 1968; setting up of the HSEP
in 1974 and the graduation quota system for colleges in 1980; and relaxing regulations on establishing new colleges in 1995.

Some of the unique features in relation to the growth and development of
Korean education would be the high aspiration and social demand for education,
the respect for teachers, overcrowded classrooms, bad educational conditions, fast-
growing advancement rates among students, a large number of private schools
requiring private funding, and so on.

Educational conditions—including classrooms, teachers, and unit costs—have
improved considerably in primary and secondary schools, even though they are
inferior to those in advanced countries. Since the latter half of the 1990s, the ratio
of public educational expenditure to GDP rose sharply, approaching the average
ratios in OECD countries, and the share of private burden for education has been
far greater than that in developed countries, maintaining Korea's prime position in
the world.

Korean education has not been able to avoid the criticism that it has pursued
quantitative expansion at the cost of qualitative deterioration. But the PISA analyses conducted by OECD reveal that Korea has been ranked at the top in educational performance in recent years.

Though the country's high level of education has not been a sufficient condition
for economic growth, the growth of education in Korea has provided its economy
with an important necessary condition for producing a sufficient and high quality
workforce.

According to empirical studies, Korean educational growth was a response to
social demand rather than manpower requirements, and approximately 0.7 % of
annual GDP growth rate could be ascribed to the contribution of education since
the 1960s, as shown in Table 7.9.

Table 7.9 Contribution of labor to economic growth (in percent)

Year	Quantitative contribution	Qualitative contribution	Total
1966–1970	3.13	0.71	3.84
1970–1975	2.68	0.68	3.36
1980–1994	1.70	0.79	2.49

Source Choi (1997)

References

Choi, K.-S. (1997). The Contribution of education to economic growth [in Korean]. *The Journal of Economics and Finance in Education, 6*(1), 59–63.

Denison, E. F. (1966). Measuring the contribution of education to economic growth. In E.A.G Robinson & J. E. Vaizey (Eds.), *The economics of education*. New York, NY: St. Martin's Press.

Jeong, C.-Y. (1977). Rates of return on investment in education. In C.-K. Kim (Ed.), *Industrial and social development issues* (p. 1977). Korea Development Institute: Seoul.

Kim, J.-E. (1973a). *An analysis of the national planning process for educational development in the republic of Korea, 1945–1970*. Unpublished doctoral dissertation, University of Pittsburgh.

Kim, S.-B. (1973b). *A systemic sub-optimization model for educational planning, with reference to Korea*. Unpublished doctoral dissertation, University of Pittsburgh.

Kim, S.-B. (1996). Education and economic development in Korea. *The Korean Journal of Policy Studies, 11*, 1–12.

Korean Educational Administration Society. (2003). *Economics of education*. Seoul: KEAS.

Korean Educational Development Institute. (2010). *Statistical yearbook of education*. Seoul: Korean Educational Development Institute.

Lee, C.-J. (2005, May). *Pro-poor education policies in Korea: Fifty years of experience*. Paper presented at regional policy seminar, in collaboration with the World Bank Institute, Beijing.

Lee, C.-J., Kim, S.-Y., & Adams, D. (Eds.). (2010). *Sixty years of korean education*. Seoul: Seoul National University Press.

McGinn, N. F., Snodgrass, D. R., Kim, Y. B., Kim, S.-B., & Kim, Q.-Y. (1980). *Education and development in Korea*. Cambridge, MA: Harvard University Press.

Ministry of Education. (2000). *Education in Korea, 2000–2001*. Seoul: Ministry of Education.

Ministry of Education and Human Resources Development. (2001). *The 100 MAJOR educational reforms of the People's government*. Seoul: Ministry of Education and Human Resources Development.

Organisation for Economic Co-operation and Development. (2002). *Education Policy Analysis 2002*. Paris: Organisation for Economic Co-operation and Development.

Organization for Economic Co-operation and Development (2000). Programme for International Student Assessment report.

Organization for Economic Co-operation and Development (2003). Programme for International Student Assessment report.

Organization for Economic Co-operation and Development (2006). Programme for International Student Assessment report.

Organization for Economic Co-operation and Development (2009). Programme for International Student Assessment report.

Paik, H.-K. (1969). *A content analysis of the elementary school textbooks and a related study for improvement of textbook administration*. Seoul: Central Education Research Institute.

Song, Byung-Nak. (2003). *The rise of the Korean economy* (3rd ed.). New York, NY: Oxford University Press.

United Nations Educational Scientific and Cultural Organization. (1974). *Republic of Korea: Educational services in a rapidly growing economy*. Paris: United Nations Educational, Scientific and Cultural Organization.

Brief Introduction

Yong-duck Jung

Professor, Graduate School of Public Administration, Seoul National University

Yong-duck Jung is a professor at Seoul National University and president of Korean Social Science Research Council. He was visiting fellow at London School of Economics and Free University of Berlin, and served as president of the Korean Association for Public Administration and Korea Institute of Public Administration, and council member of the IPSA's Research Committee on Globalization and Governance and the ASPA's Section on Chinese Public Administration. He has acted at the editorial board of *Governance, International Public Management Journal, Korean Journal of Policy Studies* (editor) and *Korean Public Administration Review* (editor). He has consulted as member of Presidential Committee for Administrative Reform and Organizing Committee for the 6th Global Forum on Reinventing Government, and co-chair with Prime Minister of Government Performance Evaluation Committee. He has written and edited many books, including *The State Apparatuses in Korea and Japan* and *Collaborative Governance in the United States and Korea.*

[Address] Graduate School of Public Administration, Seoul National University, Seoul 151-742, Republic of Korea
[Office] 82-2-880-5627
[E-mail] ydjung@snu.ac.kr

Byung-Sun Choi

Professor, Graduate School of Public Administration, Seoul National University
Byung-Sun Choi is a professor at the Graduate School of Public Administration, Seoul National University. He received his doctoral degree in Public Policy at Harvard University. He founded the Korea Society for Regulatory Studies, and headed the Korea Association of Policy Studies. He served for the Regulatory Reform Committee of the Government of Korea as its Chairman, concomitantly with the Prime Minister, during 2009–2010.
Among others, he wrote two Korean textbooks, entitled *Studies on Government Regulation* and *The Political Economy of Trade Policy*.
[Address] Graduate School of Public Administration, Seoul National University, Seoul 151-742, Republic of Korea
[Office] 82-2-880-5632
[E-mail] bschoi1@snu.ac.kr

Tobin Im

Professor, Graduate School of Public Administration, Seoul National University
Tobin Im is a professor at the Graduate School of Public Administration of the Seoul National University, South Korea. His teaching and research are in the fields of Public Organization, Comparative Administration, and Government Competitiveness. He has published extensively books and academic articles in the world class journals such as *Journal of Public Administration Research and Theory*, *American Review of Public Administration*, *Public Administration Review*, etc. He is currently researching on how to measure and improve government competitiveness from a time perspective.
[Address] Graduate School of Public Administration, Seoul National University, Seoul 151-742, Republic of Korea
[Office] 82-2-880-5615
[E-mail] tobin@snu.ac.kr

Huck-ju Kwon

Professor, Graduate School of Public Administration, Seoul National University

Huck-ju Kwon is a professor at Graduate School of Public Administration, Seoul National University. He is the Deputy Director of the Asia Development Institute at the School. He is also Director of the Global Research Network on Social Protection in East Asia, funded by the Korea Research Council. He has served for Global Social Policy as Regional Editor for East Asia since 2003 and has been Vice-President of the Research Committee 19 of International Sociological Association on Poverty, and Social Welfare and Social Policy since 2010. He also worked at the United Nations Research Institute for Social Development. His publications include, *The Korean State and Social Policy* (Oxford University 2011), *Transforming the Developmental Welfare State in East Asia* (Palgrave 2005), and *The East Asian Welfare Model: the State and Welfare Orientalism* (Routledge 1998). He has also published a number of peer review journal articles including, 'Introduction: Social Policy and Economic Development in Late Industrializers', (*International Journal of Social Welfare* 2009), 'Policy Learning and Transfer in the East Asian Developmental State' (*Policy and Politics* 2009). Kwon was awarded D.Phil in Politics from Oxford University.

[Address] Graduate School of Public Administration, Seoul National University, Seoul 151-742, Republic of Korea
[Office] 82-2-880-2621
[E-mail] hkwon4@snu.ac.kr

Min Gyo Koo

Associate Professor, Graduate School of Public Administration, Seoul National University

Min Gyo Koo is an associate professor in the Graduate School of Public Administration at Seoul National University. He is the author of a book *Island Disputes and Maritime Regime Building in East Asia: Between a Rock and a Hard Place* (2009, Springer). He is also the co-editor (with Vinod K. Aggarwal) of a book *Asia's New Institutional Architecture: Evolving Structures for Managing Trade, Financial, and Security Relations* (2007, Springer). Aside from many book chapters, he has published his research in a wide range of internationally recognized journals, including *The Pacific Review*, *International Relations of the Asia-Pacific*, *Pacific Affairs*, *Asian Perspective*, *European Journal of East Asia Studies*, and *Journal of East Asian Studies*.

[Address] Graduate School of Public Administration, Seoul National University, Seoul 151-742, Republic of Korea
[Office] 82-2-880-8535
[E-mail] mgkoo@snu.ac.kr

Shin-Bok Kim

 Emeritus Professor, Graduate School of Public Administration, Seoul National University
Shin-Bok Kim is a professor emeritus in the Graduate School of Public Administration at Seoul National University. He is the co-author of a book, *Education and Economic Development in the Republic of Korea* (1980, Harvard University Press). Aside from several English papers in Korea Journal of Policy Studies, he has published numerous articles and book chapters in Korean in the fields such as educational administration, human resource policy and management, and development planning.
[Address] Graduate School of Public Administration, Seoul National University, Seoul 151-742, Republic of Korea
[Office] 82-2-880-5618
[E-mail] sbkim1@snu.ac.kr

CPSIA information can be obtained
at www.ICGtesting.com
Printed in the USA
LVOW06s0705160717
541500LV00002B/2/P